TIRE TREADS UP MY BACK

How to Start at the Bottom and End Up Running the Place

PETER MICHAEL COLLINS

An Original Publication From Peter Michael Collins

Tire Treads Up My Back
How I Started at the Bottom and Ended Up Running the Place
Formatted by Frostbite Publishing
Copyright © 2016 by Colleen Kaye Collins
All rights reserved.

***

No part of this book may be used or reproduced without written consent from the copright holder. Thank you for respecting the hard work of this author.

***

To my Beloved Wife Colleen, Soul Mate, Fellow Adventurer, and Matriarch of our Family; our Children: Joseph, Timothy, and Cathleen; and our Granddaughters Elise and Bridget. Thank you for all that you are.

TIRE TREADS UP MY BACK

How to Start at the Bottom and
End Up Running the Place

PETER MICHAEL COLLINS

Preface

If at first the idea is not absurd, then there is no hope for it.
　　　　　Albert Einstein[1], (1879-1955)

"Anything of any significance is overdetermined. Everything worth thinking about has more than one cause."
"For any single thing of importance, there are multiple reasons."
　　　　　M. Scott Peck M.D.[2], (1936-2005)

　　My intent in writing this book was to pass on to others, who might be interested, my personal work experience and conclusions derived from my observations, as a student of, and participant in, the craft of management for more than 46 years. My work experience, excluding my military service, was in the areas of industrial manufacturing and heavy industrial construction.

　　This book is not a handbook, nor a scientific book, (although scientific principles are presented as a basis for consideration), nor even a formal study of management strategy, but rather an overview of management concepts, principles, and fundamentals at the tactical operational level. The application of the management principles and fundamentals presented in this book are not covered herein, as application is dependent upon numerous factors such as size and type of the organization for example. While my experience was in manufacturing and heavy construction, the information presented is applicable to all business, government, and religious organizations provided they have not become bureaucracies.

The underlying basic principles of management have apparently passed into obscurity. Ask yourselves: Are you satisfied with the goods and service you receive today; the attitude of the people who are supposed to serve you; the response to your valid complaints regarding poor service, or shoddy goods? When was the last time you made a telephone call for service and had the opportunity to speak directly to a customer service representative without having to spend several minutes punching in a series of numbers before you were connected to a human being? Interestingly enough, such organizations have the arrogance and audacity to call this "Customer Service." Personally, I find the devaluation of the worth of my time by such companies or agencies, with which I am trying to do business, to be an insult.

According to Peter Drucker[3], "A business exists to create

a customer." So whatever happened to the old idea that if you treat the customer right, the customer will return to buy your product or services? We have increasingly become a throwaway society. Buy a throwaway digital camera, take the pictures and then throw the camera away. We seem to treat customers the same way. Repeat customers are no longer sought. So the customer is treated badly? Another customer will show up! The long established idea that satisfied customers were a desirable goal was lost in the implementation of technology for technologies' sake by the unknowing, the unthinking, and the uncaring. There is not, nor will there ever be, a substitute for service, and recognition of customers needs and desires by companies who aspire to success over the long term.

In the course of my own working career, I have witnessed the changes that have resulted in the deterioration in the management function from a series of skill sets to a mere position title. The ability to manage effectively has been lost in the present era. Management is a function, not an event or title. Organizations commonly assign the title of "Manager" to employees who have little or no training, little or no experience, and generally no idea of the basic principles and functions inherent in the management process. Therefore, to these so-called managers and their superiors, the mission of management assumes the place of a subordinate role in the daily scheme of work related priorities, and is usually associated with the performances of a single event, or of some routine administrative chores. **In reality, the primary purpose of a manager is to manage. Management is a full time occupation, as will be presented in this book.**

The purpose of this book then, is to re-identify the fundamental principles governing the management function. This book will explore, in some detail, the areas of: Process, Universal Principles, Organization, Focus, Communication, and Discipline. Additionally, the presentation will identify factors that can positively or negatively affect employees' performance. Becoming aware of these factors and addressing their consequences can lead to the establishment of a creative work environment for the employees. Organizations are all about people. Change the mindset of employees from negative, or even neutral, to positive and you have embraced a formula for the success of your business.

I ask the readers to evaluate, through their own experience, the efficacy of the information that I have presented. My hope is that the book will, at the very least, have encouraged you the reader to explore further some of the ideas identified in this book.

P. M. Collins
Prescott Valley
Arizona, 2008

Introduction

If you are going to sin, sin against God, not the bureaucracy God will forgive you, but the bureaucracy won't.
Hyman G. Rickover[1] (1900-1986)

Where is the life we have lost in living? Where is the wisdom we have lost in knowledge? Where is the knowledge we have lost in information?"
T. S. Eliot[2] (1888-1965)

CONCEPT: *n.* 2. A broad abstract idea or a guiding general principle, such as one that determines how a person or culture behaves, or how nature, reality, or events are perceived.

FUNDAMENTAL: *adj.* 1. Relating to or affecting the underlying principles or structure of something.

PRINCIPLE: *n.* 4. A basic or essential quality or element determining intrinsic nature or

characteristic behavior.

As the title of this book would suggest, bureaucracies are excluded from consideration in this book. Bureaucracies are governed by their own set of laws which I have summed up as follows: *A bureaucracy exists for its own sake, therefore all decisions made by the bureaucrats, firstly and foremost, are made based on the requirement to sustain and enlarge the bureaucracy.* <u>The purpose for which any bureaucracy was initially created is soon lost with the passage of time.</u> Pick any bureaucracy: business, government, religious, etc., for analysis and decide for yourself. The approach taken in this book is to look at the organization, whether business, government, religious, etc., and treat the non-bureaucratic organization as a system, while exploring the processes that govern systems. (The examples used in this book will focus on business systems specifically, although the terms, e.g., business, organization, company, etc., may be used interchangeably throughout the book.)

I believe that the topics and material presented in this book have the greatest relevance to organizations and/or units within organizations comprised of no more than 150 people[3]. Above that number the organization, be it business, government, church, etc., has likely metamorphosed into the bureaucratic mode, and the laws of bureaucracy then govern that organization. However, even within a bureaucracy there may be the opportunity, at the department and group levels for application of the fundamentals delineated in this book.

The time in which we live is often called the "Age of Information". In the style of Winston Churchill, *Never has so much information meant so little, to so many!* In our culture today, information has taken the place of knowledge; formal education the place of training and experience; events the place of processes; and arrogance the place of understanding.

In order to be successful in the future, a business must be run in accord with universal principles. Scientists tell us today that all events occurring in the universe are part of a process. A major component of the problems that we are currently experiencing in the business world, in government, religious, and social organizations is the result of ignoring this fundamental truth. The impact of new technology on all these organizations, and the tendency to place such a high reliance on technology as a panacea to all problems that arise in the course of the day has resulted in the diminishing of the value of the personnel who make up an organization by those who are in charge.

There has been insufficient time and attention paid to keep pace with the rapid changes resulting from the swift advance of the latest information technology. Experience, which only comes with the passage of time, must be accumulated before the standards, systems and procedures required for stability in the arena of advanced technology can be developed and promulgated. For new technology to be of real benefit, these changes must be in place. In the interim, we are operating under the fallacious assumption that new technology, in and by itself, will solve problems.

Technology is merely a tool. The mystique of "technology" not only has resulted in our abandonment of fundamental principles, decline of creative thinking, and the loss of problem solving skills, but also has deluded us into believing that all the answers to life's problems can be resolved through and by technology. This thinking throughout history has proved illusionary. Over the long term, success for any organization truly results from reliance on the focused effort and creative capabilities of the people working there. To the degree that an enterprise relies, in great part, on new technology to deal with the problems encountered in daily operational activities rather than its people, the enterprise will ultimately suffer and decline. It is people who solve problems, which have ultimately resulted from the consequences of peoples' decisions and actions in the first place. (It is unfortunate that the study of history no longer has a pre-eminent place in our public school educational curriculum today.)

I have heard this statement made countless times over the years, "People are our most important resource", by those supposedly in charge, who have no idea as to the responsibilities they have inherent in their positions of authority to ensure that the employees under their authority receive all the resources required to perform their assigned tasks. Those in charge have the obligation to make sure their employees are well treated physically, mentally, emotionally, and economically. The best information, the best management strategy and tactics, the best marketing plans, and the best equipment, etc., will not assure optimum performance within an organization, unless the people who work in that organization are valued and treated accordingly.

In our culture today, the tendency seems to be to treat every occurrence as it were an event, rather than as part of a process. This leads to the specious conclusion that if we can explain this event in simplistic terms at the superficial level, or in the case of a problem, at the symptomatic level, then we have an immediate understanding of the significance and consequence(s) of the event, or again, as in the case of a problem, we have one fix that will make this problem go away. However, if the view of an occurrence is one of process determination and understanding that there are a number of universal laws, which inherently govern all processes, then making overly simplistic determinations of cause and affect can be avoided, thereby avoiding the long-term consequences of such simplistic thinking.

This book then is written on the premise that every business is, in fact a "system", and that the dynamics of systems are process oriented. Furthermore, every process is governed by Universal Laws. Regarding business systems, I have addressed three Universal Laws that appear to have a significant impact on business systems: "Entropy"; The Pereto Principle, i.e., The 80/20 Rule; and Parkinson's Law. Failure to recognize, and pay heed to the impact of these three laws has resulted in many businesses today appearing to operate according to the principle: "It's Just Whatever Happens", or more succinctly, on the basis that the consequences are the cause.

Another concept presented in this book is that of the "Critical Zone". The "Critical Zone", as I define it for the purpose of this book, is the primary area in a business entity where the core income is generated. There may be subsets to the primary area, depending on the business process flow, but there will be only one Critical Zone. This concept will be discussed further in Chapter Two.

Let us now move on to the subject matter. The discussion of Processes and Universal Laws will form the basis for the presentation of all of the information that is to follow. The emphasis in the Processes Section of Chapter One, is on people: How we observe and react, how we learn, and how our individual experiences influence how we perform. Organizations are about people dealing with people. To reiterate, many modern day businesses consign people to the lowest point of worth in the system. Contrary to the popular saying, Ignorance is not bliss! Ignorance of the human condition is totally counterproductive to achieving meaningful success in the business world, always was, always will be. The Wall Street criterion of short-term profit as the measure of success of a company is delusional, always was always, will be.

Please Note: The specific word definitions used in this book, unless otherwise noted, are taken from: *The AMERICAN HERITAGE dictionary of THE ENGLISH LANGUAGE, fourth edition ©; or the ENCARTA® WORLD ENGLISH DICTIONARY, 1999 © by Microsoft Corporation.* The number shown in the word definition is the Dictionary's sequence number for that definition.

Chapter One
Processes

PROCESS: *n.* **1. a series of actions, changes, or functions bringing about a result. (*A Process is characterized by continuous change, activity, or progress over time.*)**

SYSTEM: *n.* **1. a group of interacting, interrelated, or interdependent elements forming a complex whole 4. a social, economic, or political organizational form**

All business entities are systems. As identified previously in the **INTRODUCTION,** scientists today tell us that everything that exists in the Universe is part of a process. Processes govern systems. Universal laws govern processes. The unfortunate aspect of our Western culture is that this truth is not fully recognized. It would appear that enterprises today operate with the view that everything that happens is a separate event and therefore is to be dealt with as an individual occurrence, (even though it may be of a repetitive nature).

How did we get lost? We continue to forget what was already known! George Santayana[1] has said: "Those who cannot remember the past are doomed to repeat it." In order to avoid this disconnect, we would have to study the past, not only remember the past, but use the lessons of the past as the *pathway to the future*. Unfortunately for all of us, studying the past, in general, is not a cultural prerogative in this day and age. Perhaps the hubris of modern man is such that he believes that what he is experiencing has never happened before, and therefore he is totally unique.

We have forgotten how to think! George Bernard Shaw[2] was quoted as saying: "Few people think more than two or three times per year. I have made an international reputation for myself by thinking once or twice a week." Today we are not educated to think. We are educated as to what to think, i.e., the collection and memorization of information. Technology has replaced the need to think! Technology has forced us into specialization to the degree that we have developed tunnel vision and have lost sight of the whole!

Are these unrelated occurrences? No. These events are governed by Fundamental Universal Principles. **It is the failure to recognize and adhere to these Fundamental Universal Principles that has brought us to our present state of disorder.**

We will first look at three different processes: WISDOM, TRUTH, and LEARNING.

_____

THE WISDOM PROCESS PYRAMID
Comments & Definitions

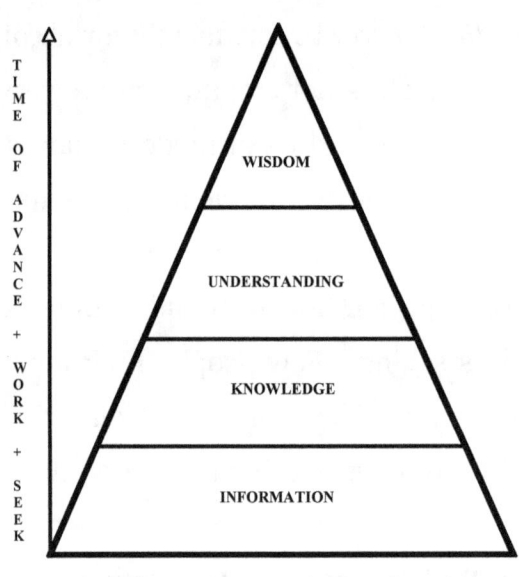

Illustration 1-1

WISDOM: *n.* **1. the ability to see what is true, right, or lasting insight**

UNDERSTANDING: *n.* **1. the perception and comprehension of the nature and significance of**

understanding evolves from the reflection upon individual knowledge gained relevant to a specific standard or code, e.g., spiritual, moral code, system of ethics, industry standard, etc.

KNOWLEDGE: *n.* **3. the sum or range of what has been perceived, discovered, or learned.**

Knowledge is empirical: "Life is lived going forward, and learned looking backwards."

INFORMATION: *n.* **3. a collection of facts or data.**

Information, in and by itself, i.e., if not incorporated into action, or put to use, is essentially without value.

It is interesting to note that as we progress upward in the hierarchy of the Wisdom Process Pyramid, Illustration 1-1, and for that matter all of the process transitions, we are unable to fully assimilate all that has occurred in the previous level.

When I was 12 years old, I had convinced myself that I could drive our newly purchased family car which had a manual transmission. I had read and memorized the "information" which was provided in the car Owner's

Manual. I finally badgered my Father into letting me get in the new car for my first attempt at driving. The car was in the driveway along side of the house. I started the engine, put the car in reverse and proceeded to jerk the car across the lawn, narrowly missing a rather large elm tree by the curb, and came jerking to a halt crosswise in the street. Fortunately there was no traffic. My Father and I emerged from the car, shaken but unhurt. Since then I have spent the last 54 years learning how to drive a car in all conditions!

The moral of this story is that I had sufficient "information" about how to drive the car out of the driveway, but having no experience in driving a car, I had no knowledge and therefore no understanding of how to drive.

This same mistake is made in our business world today when education is deemed an acceptable substitute for experience and training. By the way, we get about the same results in business as I did trying to drive a car in my ignorance: the whole thing eventually comes jerking to a stop. In a business, it may just take longer!

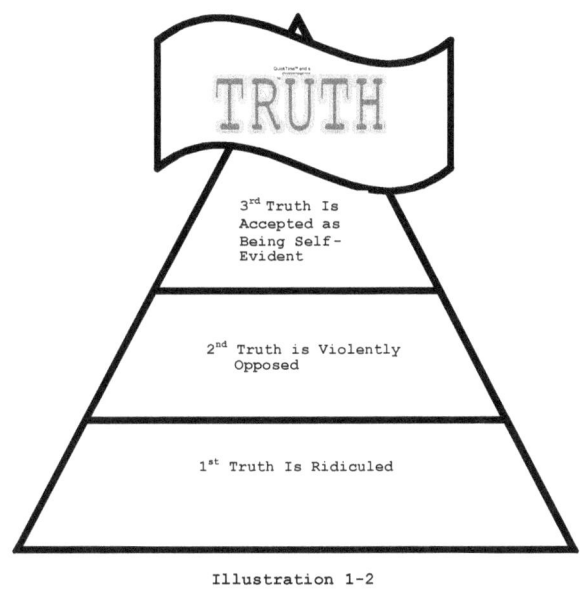

Illustration 1-2

(Quote Above by Arthur Shopenhauer[3])

"All great truths begin as blasphemies."[4]
George Bernard Shaw[4]

"Beware of False Knowledge; it is more dangerous than ignorance."
George Bernard Shaw[5]

TRUTH: conformity to fact or actuality

The question before us is: Why is it so difficult to arrive at the truth? Cultural influences notwithstanding, the problem rests in our failure to understand that arriving at the truth is not obtaining or being presented with information, but rather progressing through the process from initial exposure to the truth, to ultimate acceptance of the truth. The journey from exposure to acceptance is the process previously identified in the *WISDOM Process Pyramid*. The *WISDOM Process Pyramid* and the *TRUTH Process Pyramid,* Illustration 1-2, are congruent processes, linked not sequentially, but concurrently. In other words it is the same journey, the same path traveled.

There is a psychological term called "cognitive dissonance[6]" which identifies the "discomfort felt at a discrepancy between what you already know or believe, and new information or interpretation" which engenders a need to accommodate new ideas. This dichotomy is oftentimes very emotionally painful and often has the unfortunate consequence of forcing an individual either to be open to the new idea(s), or to defend his/her original position because the person knows that he/she is "right", and therefore you, whoever you are, are "wrong". A quick look at the political ideology, etc., prevalent in our society today will provide all the graphic proof of this you might need to verify that cognitive dissonance abounds. Herbert Spencer[7] described our current cultural perspective thusly: "There is a principle which is a bar against all information, which is proof against all arguments and which cannot fail to keep a man in everlasting ignorance---that principle is contempt prior to investigation."

(It is perhaps interesting to note an oft-misquoted passage from the Bible, John 8:32: *"and the truth shall set you free,"* whereas the passage actually reads: ***"and you shall know the truth**, and the truth shall set you free."* The operative word here is *know*, a stage in the process.)

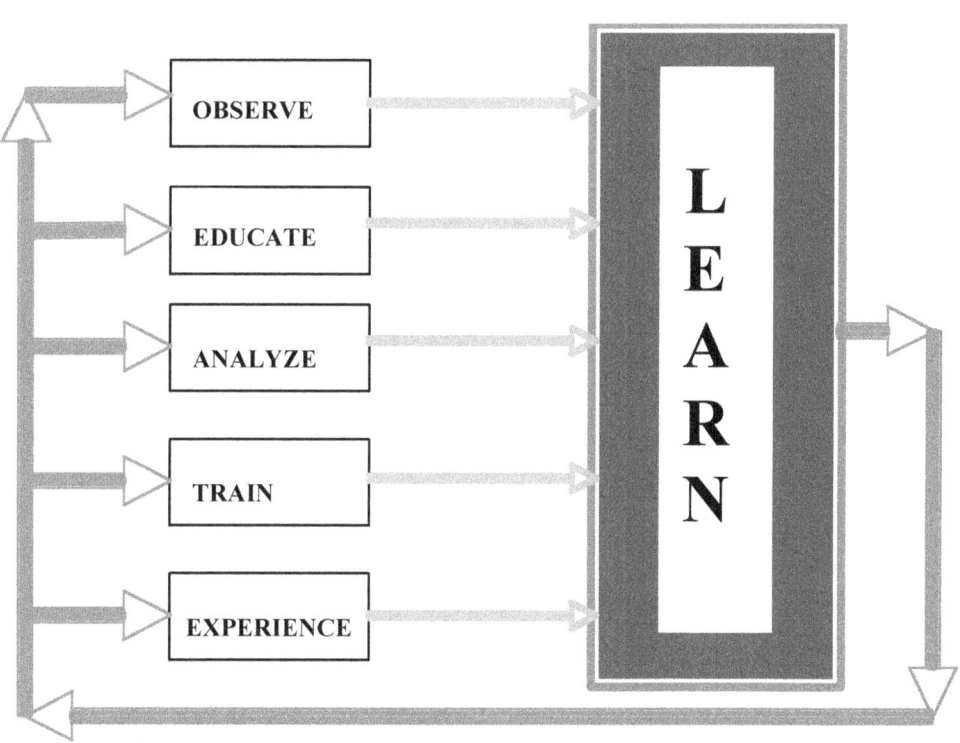

Illustration 1-3

ELEMENTS OF LEARNING:

LEARN: *v.* **1.** to gain knowledge, comprehension, or mastery of through experience or study

OBSERVE: *v.* **1.** to be or become aware of, especially through careful and directed attention

EDUCATE: *v.* **1.** to develop the innate capacities of, especially by schooling or instruction

ANALYZE: *tr.v.* **1.** to examine methodically by separating into parts and studying their interrelations

TRAIN: *tr.v.* **1.** to make proficient with specialized instruction and practice

EXPERIENCE: n. 2a. active participation in events or activities, leading to the accumulation of knowledge or skill

THE LEARNING PROCESS:

In all my years of taking Management Courses, attending Management Seminars, and reading articles on Management, I do not recall coming across any discussion about the learning process of people as it directly and specifically relates to the management function.

Business enterprises are all about people, and yet we do not address this fundamental issue of learning as it impacts the business environment. If, in fact, people are not viewed as being the most valuable resource existent in an organization, no matter what the type and structure of the organization, then people are likely to be viewed as being only an abstract company resource which demands no further evaluation of the individual than that the individual is counted on the organization's rolls.

Does learning cease when an individual attains the level of formal education deemed necessary to provide access to the job to which the individual aspires? Unfortunately, in this day and age, it appears so. Should learning actually cease? No! Does learning, (not education which is only one component of the learning process), receive the emphasis it deserves in the daily activities of a business enterprise today? Again, the answer is no!

A business entity will grow and prosper only to the extent that the people who make up the organization, at all levels, grow and prosper as well. It is of the utmost importance that individuals who hold management positions have a basic understanding of the makeup of this most basic human process: Learning.

As shown in Illustration 1-3, the five major elements of learning are hierarchal with feedback loops. Let us now view, in turn, each of these elements in sequence, while keeping in mind that my presentation of information is an overview only, and addresses these elements in a general way.

Educators tell us that the more senses we call into play in learning, the more thoroughly we are likely to learn the object of study, and the longer we are likely to remember what we have learned. Although the five senses may play a role in our learning, (through observation), the combination of seeing and hearing seems to predominate, independent of which of these two senses is the primary sense for each individual.

OBSERVATION:

When we receive information visually, what does the eye see? It is well known scientifically, that the eye has a *blind spot*[8] which results from a lack of light-sensitive rods and cones in the retina. One school of thought suggests that what we see is not what appears on the retina, but that the brain's visual cortex fills in the blind spot, and perhaps reprocesses the entire visual field. If this is the case, then we do not get what we see, but instead we get created information. "The world that we see is not something out there, but a world that we invent." "The world I see is my idea.[9]"

In looking at another of the factors that influence what we observe, we will look to John R. Boyd's OODA LOOP[10]. (Boyd's OODA LOOP will be presented in Chapter Six), When we consider the impact of the Blind Spot Phenomenon and the OODA LOOP Process on how we, as humans, observe events as they are unfolding before us, we can conclude that each individual's observation of events unfolding before him/her is *unique* to that individual. (Isn't it interesting to note how much trouble occurs in the world as a result of the need for individuals/organizations to convince others that what they see is "right' and therefore, if you disagree with them, you are wrong?) Please keep in mind, that how we observe will have a direct influence on the remaining four elements of learning process.

The only thing that interferes with my learning is my education.
Albert Einstein[11]

EDUCATION:

As a general statement, public school education in this country today does not sufficiently prepare an individual for meaningful employment in the work force. A large majority of Public High School graduates, we are told today, cannot read or perform basic mathematics at a reasonable level required for success in the workforce. At the elementary school level there is a continual shift away from the fundamentals of reading, writing, and arithmetic in favor of the teaching of computer skills. Technology is replacing the focus on development of basic skills at the entrance level of education. I had occasion one day to experience two separate instances, where, when making purchases under $20.00 in each case, the sales clerks having to use the old fashion non-computer type cash register were unable to correctly determine the exact change due to me. In both instances the clerks appeared to be old enough to be high school graduates. They appeared bright, personable, and eager to please. These employees were without the basic math skills to function in a place of business that lacked the technology commonly used today in most retail establishments.

At the college level, the curriculum is often conceptual in nature rather than reflecting the reality of the workplace. While theory is important, it must be accompanied by practical information, which will prepare the individual for entrance into, and/or meaningful advancement in the workplace. (We will explore the topic of Education further in Chapter Three, the section on Hiring.)

ANALYZATION:

Regarding Analysis, "Our Educational System today teaches students "what to think, instead of how to think."

This is the result of a number of cultural factors present in our society today.

The current frenzied pace of our society today drives us into the point of view that the passage of time is our enemy. Accordingly, our busyness becomes the requirement, and in order to accommodate our busyness we do not take the time to observe, analyze or think, and we let others do the observing, analyzing and thinking for us. Compounding this, in the information age, the sheer volume of information that surrounds us, overpowers us. However, a great deal of this information is pre-digested for us by others and presented to us as fact. The television media *sound bite* has conditioned us to watch and listen instead of think. The scrolling of information at the bottom of the television is a further distraction implying that we are to read and listen at the same time. I identify this phenomenon as multi-tasking which, translated means doing more than one thing at a time. Multi-tasking appears to me to be the great bane of our society. If genius is manifest by the ability to focus intently on only one thing at a time in order to do it very well, then multi-tasking is the distraction that drives us to deal with multiple things at the same time, and do them all poorly.

This is the society that we live in today. In the business community, failure to recognize the forces that exist in the specific business entity in which we are involved is tantamount to calling up a friend and asking directions to their house, and in response to their inquiry: Where are you? You reply, I don't know. If you don't know where you are, there is no way to get to where you want to go. Or in the business system, if you don't know the wind and the currents that are propelling the ship, how are you going to be able to steer the ship to its proper destination? The answer lies in embracing and implementing the common sense fundamentals of Management in the day to day running of the business.

TRAINING:

In my experience the most glaring deficiency of organizations is the failure to adequately train their employees. There are two notable and obvious exceptions: the military and sports teams. Why don't businesses train their employees, except when training is unavoidable, e.g., ISO9000, which is a collection of quality management standards from the International Organization for Standardization. ISO Certification is generally required for Business Organizations to sell their products overseas. I believe that there are two major factors in play here: The "Fallacy of Education", and the "Up front cost of training is too expensive."

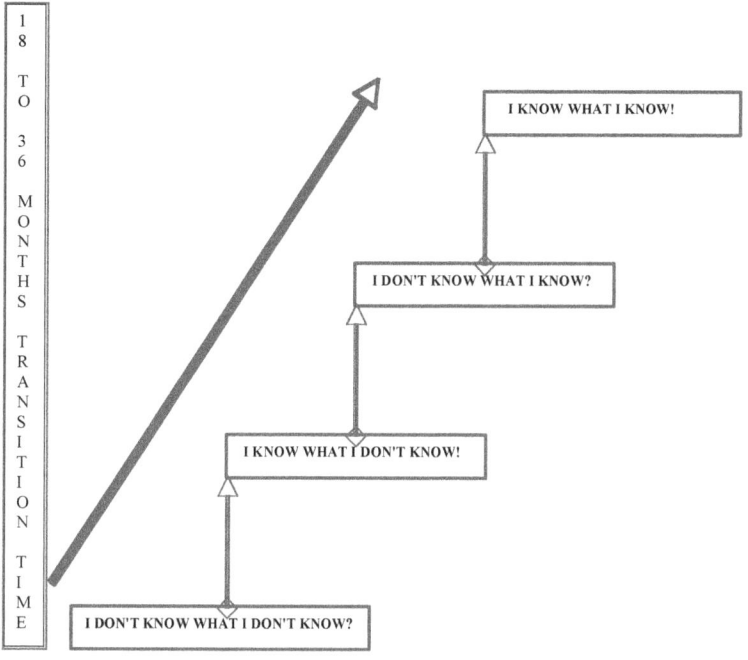

Illustration 1-4

The fallacy of education is the belief that a general education, at whatever level required for entrance to an employment position, eliminates the need to train an individual to perform specific job functions. The belief seems to be that the employees, after a brief exposure to the position, will pick up the necessary skills by working at their position. The only thing employees will pick up over time, without specific training, is bad habits. A look at the "Progression of Learning Process", Illustration 1-4, identifies that after an 18-36 month time period, the individual employee, having arrived at Level 4, "Will Know What

He/She Knows". This does not mean that the employee will know what he/she should know. The certainty is, that without proper training, the employee will most likely not be in a position to meet the goals and objectives of the organization. (The employee, in effect, is expected to take a knife to a gunfight!)

Business decisions today are made disproportionately on the basis of financial considerations, at the expense of operational requirements. (Ref. Critical Zone discussion later in Chapter 1.) The up front cost of training is too expensive, the aforementioned second factor. Therefore the organization cannot afford the required training at this time. This shortsighted view, coupled with the Fallacy of Education, results in training being considered "nice to have", rather than the imperative that it actually is. The truth of the matter is that without proper training, the cost of untrained employees is lost in hidden costs resulting from: inefficiency, lost productivity, poor quality, customer dissatisfaction, and employee dissatisfaction. Over time, these hidden costs often far exceed the up front cost of training. Since these costs are hidden, these costs never come to the attention of management. They appear as a lump sum in overhead.

Another aspect of training that is overlooked by those responsible for the stability and growth of the organization, is that training and individual creativity go hand in hand.

Individual creativity can only emerge and grow in the well-trained and properly motivated employee! Failure to recognize this fundamental truth will always result in an irreplaceable loss of creative energy to the organization.

———————

EXPERIENCE:

Experience can be separated into two categories: Open or Closed. Open Experience is present when an individual has the perspective that life and learning are dynamic and progressive, and understands and accepts the fact that there is something new to be learned from situations and events as they occur each day. This person has a positive outlook and will continue to grow all of their life as long as this attitude is maintained. Contrast this view with the individual who is locked into the category of Closed Experience. This individual having a negative, outlook attains some desired goal in life such as graduation from college, or reaching a certain level in the workforce, etc., and ceases to grow as an individual from that point on. Many such individuals become critics of life instead of living life. These individuals have a detrimental influence on the organizational environment and, as such, will always be a hindrance to the stability and growth of the organization.

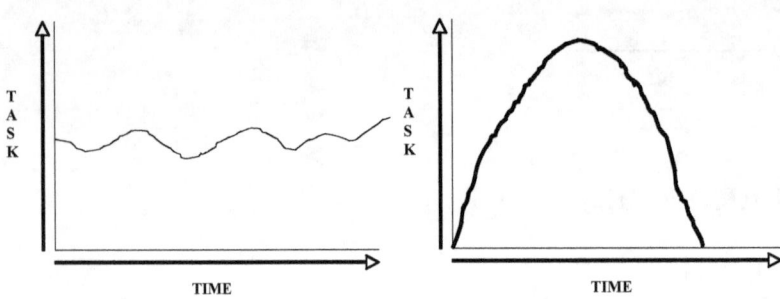

Illustration 1-5 Illustration 1-6

The type of work employees perform shapes their individual work perspectives. The purpose of Illustrations 1-5, and 1-6, is to contrast the difference in the work perspective of employees whose work efforts are directed in support of tasks with a limited variable range, repetitive in nature, (Illustration 1-5), versus employees whose work is project oriented. Project tasks are non-repetitive in nature, and contain a large number of variables. Illustration 1-6 shows that a project begins at the Task Zero Point, progresses upward to the peak, and descends over time back to the Task Zero Point as shown. A manager responsible for a manufacturing operation would tend to have a Horizontal Perspective relating to that type of operation. A manager responsible for an industrial construction project would tend to have a Vertical Perspective.

It is ludicrous to expect that an individual is experienced and competent in every endeavor imaginable, and yet this happens frequently. Once again the Fallacy of Education would lead us to believe that if an individual has a degree, or better yet an advanced degree, that this, in and by itself, qualifies the individual to perform all jobs without requiring any experience or training. **It is worth repeating here that EDUCATION, by definition, is only one of the five elements of LEARNING.**

SUMMARY:

Universal Laws govern processes.

Processes govern systems.   **Process = Change**

⟹

All business entities are Systems.

Management does not understand the three processes that deal with how individuals think, learn, and understand. Yet people are the most important part of the business equation.

The Wisdom Process; The Truth Process; and The Learning Process.

are three important processes impacting businesses.

The Wisdom Process is a Four Step Progression. (Illus. 1-1)

The Truth Process is a Three Step Progression. (Illus. 1-2)

The Learning Process is Five Step, Continuous Feedback Progression. (Illus. 1-3)

The Wisdom, Truth, and Learning Processes are interrelated as shown in the VENN Diagram. (Illus. 1-7)

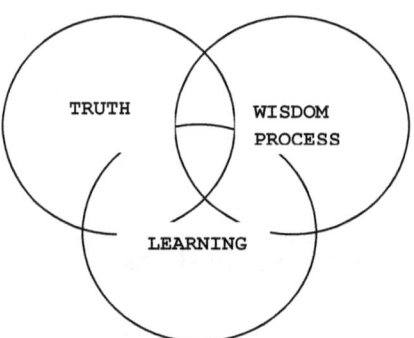

Illustration 1-7

There are Four Milestones of Learning that span an 18-36 months duration. (Illus.1-4)

The Fallacy of Education, and the Up Front Cost of Training negatively influence management's decisions on employee training.

Experience is either Open or Closed depending on the motivation of the individual.

The type of work employees perform shapes their individual work perspectives. (Illus. 1-5, 1-6)

Chapter Two
Universal Principals & the Critical Zone

A social organization can regulate only so much deviation from behavioral norms. If deviancy begins to exceed that capacity, the organization will change the standard, accepting behavior previously found objectionable.
Extracted from an 1993 essay by Daniel Patrick Moynihan[1] (1927-2003)

ENTROPY: *n*, 2. a measure of the disorder or randomness in a closed system.
3. a measure of the loss of information in a transmitted message.
5. inevitable and steady deterioration of a system or society.

The concept of entropy was developed during the industrial
revolution in the field of thermodynamics. The 2nd Law

of Thermodynamics identifies entropy as a quantitative measure of the amount of thermal energy not available to do work in a closed thermodynamic dynamic system. Outside of the field of thermodynamics, entropy now is considered a factor in all systems, e.g., Definitions 2, 3, and 5.

A common illustration used to portray the phenomenon of entropy is shown in Illustrations 2-1, and 2-2. In Illustration 2-1, the carbonation is contained within the liquid in the capped soda pop bottle. Illustration 2-2 shows the carbonation escaping to the environment in the form of tiny bubbles when the soda pop bottle is uncapped. Illustration 2-2 then, is a pictorial representation of an increase in entropy, (disorder).

I have used the words "stable system" and "unstable system", in lieu of "closed" and "open" systems, respectively, to transition the perspective for this presentation from thermodynamics to organizational systems, specifically businesses, i.e., Definition 5 above. " (I qualify the use of the word "inevitable" in Definition 5, as it relates to business systems, to be true only, if no external action, (energy), is applied to the system.)

Illustration 2-1   Illustration 2-2

Entropy: Stable System   Entropy: Unstable System

As an example, let us look at the organizational structure of a business. The organizational structure of a company is established at a point in time, (Stable System), based on the type of business, e.g., retail, manufacturing, service, etc, the region, the type of market, etc. Over time, the company expands or contracts, positions are added, eliminated, or changed, technology brings innovations such as e-mail, new accounting software, cell phones, etc. (It should be noted that technological advances have the propensity to accelerate entropy.) Yet, despite significant changes occurring within a business over time, no modifications are made to the organizational structure of the company to reflect such changes. With no attention being paid to the organizational structure, the organizational structure deteriorates in terms of purpose and function. (Unstable System). Since the organizational structure of a business is the fundamental structure upon which all other elements of the business depend, the deterioration of the organizational structure precipitates a decline in performance in all of the activities of the business. (Organization is addressed in Chapter Three.)

"Nature tends from order to disorder." Entropy is present in every facet of a business system: seven

days a week, twenty-four hours per day, three hundred and sixty five days per year. **The deleterious deterioration within the business progresses unnoticed until the crises begin to appear.** Then we hear the timeworn statement from the organization's management to the effect: "We will conduct a full investigation into this incident, and initiate corrective action to prevent such things happening in the future." (Until the next time!)

There are many examples of the effects of entropy on a company that has no mechanism in place to deal with entropy. Make your own observation on any organization over time. Expanding bureaucracies are a prime example of entropy at work.

Remember in the Preface to this book I made the following statements: **"The primary purpose of a manager is to manage." "Management is a full time occupation."** Guess who is the custodian of entropy for a business? The Manager!

"The 80/20 Principle can and should be used by every intelligent person in their daily life, by every organization, and by every social grouping and form of society. It can help individuals and groups

achieve much more, with much less effort."
Richard Koch (1950-)[2] The 80/20 Principle

In 1906, Vilfredo Pareto,[3] a French born, Italian economist and lecturer at the University of Lausanne in Switzerland, made the observation that, in Italy, twenty percent of the population owned eighty percent of the property. Pareto carried out surveys in other countries and discovered that the eighty percent-twenty percent distribution applied in those countries as well. In 1941, an American Industrial Engineer, Joseph M. Juran,[4] expanded the work of Pareto into the so-called Pareto Principle, (also known as the 80-20 Rule). Juran applied the Pareto Principle to quality issues, e.g., 80 percent of a problem is generated by 20 percent of the causes. Later on Juran's preferred view of the Pareto Principle was "The vital few, and the useful many" to signify that the remaining causes should not be completely ignored. In keeping with this idea, and my experience which has demonstrated time and again that both sides of the equation must be evaluated thoroughly in order to achieve a full understanding of the significance of the data, I chose to portray the numerical symbolism of the Pareto Principle thusly: **80 20**, (as contrasted with the usual forms: 80/20; 80-20; 80:20). ⇌

The Pareto Principle simply stated says that from a specific group of elements 20% of the elements produce 80%

of the results. Conversely, 80 percent of the elements will produce only 20 percent of the results.

Although in recent years there has been more recognition of the

Pareto Principle in the business community, this recognition has not been translated into widespread adaptation in business. I suspect that where the Pareto Principle has been utilized in companies, oftentimes, this has been limited to only one aspect of the business, e.g., sales. In fact, the Pareto Principle has universal application throughout the business's organization. We shall look further at the use of the Pareto Principle in CHAPTER FOUR of this book.

———————

Parkinson's Law: "Work Expands so as to fill the time available for its completion."
C. Northcote Parkinson (1909-1993)[5], Parkinson's Law

In 1958 C. Northcote Parkinson, a Naval Historian and Author of numerous books, wrote the book *Parkinson's Law: The Pursuit of Progress*, a satire on human behavior. The Law quoted above was just an example of many examples given by Parkinson:

Law of Triviality: The time spent on any item on the agenda will be in inverse proportion to the cost involved.

Law of Data: Data expands to fill the space available for storage.

Law of Expenditures: Expenditures rise to meet income.

Parkinson, in another of his examples, addressed the phenomenon of the expansion of the workforce without a corresponding expansion of the workload. While I believe that this particular example applies mainly to bureaucracies, nonetheless the hypothesis is relevant to all organizations, no matter what their size.

All of Parkinson's Laws are examples of entropy. Unless there is awareness that disorder is continuously taking place in the business system, and appropriate corrective action taken to offset this disorder, the business is in decline. Here again is another example of the responsibility of the manager: to have situational awareness of the dynamic forces existent in the organization and to deal with the problems engendered in a timely and efficient manner.

_____

THE CRITICAL ZONE:

Critical Zone:* The Primary Area, where, in a business system the work that produces core

income is performed or accomplished. (Think of the critical zone as being the reason the business was started in the first place, e.g., manufacture a product. The critical zone is where the product is physically produced.)

Core Income:* Income derived solely from the ultimate provision of goods and/or services to an outside entity, exclusive of any income derived from financial manipulation, or other purely financial mechanisms

(Note: * Author's definitions)

There is a rule-of-thumb relating to management, which applies relative to the Critical Zone in business systems today. The rule of thumb states: "The higher a person rises in the management hierarchy, the less he/she is aware of the operations taking place in the Critical Zone, and the greater the power and authority he/she has to control the operations within the critical zone. Or to restate this rule-of-thumb from the opposite perspective: "The more you are aware of the operational dynamics existent in the Critical Zone, the less power you have to control or change it." (This resultant has an overall detrimental effect on the AUTHORITY-RESPONSIBILITY-CONSEQUENCES PROCESS at the level of the Critical Zone.)

A simple formula and the examples below illustrate this

rule-of-thumb principle.

Formula:

One: A=C/P,

where: A = Awareness (System Operations)

C = Critical Zone. C is a constant equal to 1.

P = Management position held in the Business System*,

where the following numbers are assigned:

P = 1, Direct Supervisor

P = 2, Manager, (Department)

P = 3, Manager, (Division)

P = 4, Director

P = 5, Vice-President

P = 6, President

P = 7, CEO

P = 8, Board of Directors

(* Level in Management can be utilized instead of Position
title.)

Example: One: A=C/P, where C=1 and P=1; then where P=7

A=1/1 A=1/7

$\underline{A=1}$ $\underline{A=0.14}$

Two: P=C/A

The numerical value of "A" obtained from the Formula, One above, is to be used in Two, The Critical Zone constant"1" remains the same.

While the numerical values of "P" used in Formula One above remain the same, "P" is changed to represent "Power" instead of "Position, (or Level in Management.")

Example: Two: P=C/A, where C=1 and A=1; then where A=0.14

P=1/1 P=1/0.14

$\underline{P=1}$ $\underline{P=7.14}$

These formulas identify the need for "flat" organizational structures, as well as identify an implied argument for limiting "Span of Control" responsibilities within the organization.

The deleterious effects of the rule-of-thumb phenomenon in a System can be ameliorated by a System's Organizational Structure, Focus, Communication Procedures, and Discipline, as will be presented in the chapters to follow.

SUMMARY:

Businesses must be run according to universal principles.

Universal Laws govern businesses.
Entropy: Nature tends from order to disorder.
Pareto Principle: From a specific group of elements 20% (80 20) the elements produce 80% of the results.

Parkinson's Law: Work expands so as to fill the time available for its completion.

All of Parkinson's Laws are examples of entropy in action.

The responsibility of the Manager is to ameliorate the effects of entropic processes throughout the organization.

The Critical Zone: The primary area, where, in a business system the work that produces core income is performed or accomplished.

The Critical Zone Formula: A=C/P.

The Critical Zone Rule of Thumb: The higher a person

rises in the management hierarchy, the less he/she is aware of the operations taking place in the critical zone, and the greater the power and authority he/she has to control the operations in the critical zone.

According to the Critical Zone Formula flat organizational structures, and limited span of control are desirable.

Chapter Three
Organization

Business is not just doing deals; business is having great products, doing great engineering, and providing tremendous service to customers. Business is a cobweb of human relationships.
Ross Perot[1] (1930-)

MISSION: *n.* 1. a particular task given to a person or group to carry
out.
2. an aim or task that somebody believes it is his/her duty to carry out or to which he/she attaches special importance and devotes special care.

GOAL: *n.* 1. the purpose toward which an endeavor is directed; an objective.

A Mission Statement is a statement of purpose that defines not only the goals of an organization but the culture of the organization as well. Mission Statements are critically important. However, over the years I have observed that the Mission Statements of many organizations are poorly done, to such a degree that they are mostly ignored. In any organization, the first definition of the word MISSION shown above applies to the organization as a whole. The second definition of the word MISSION is the definition that is relevant for each individual employed in the organization. The importance of having the appropriate mission statements for an organization cannot be overemphasized. The organizational structure of a business is derived from the intent of the Mission Statements.

Several mission statements will be required for each business.

The General or Public, Mission Statement, will be determined by the nature of the business, e.g., Construction, Manufacturing, Retail, Service, etc. The very nature of the General Mission Statement normally requires that it not be specific and detailed in order to accommodate a broad client base.

Each business must also have several Internal Mission Statements, down to the level of the individual employee. These internal Mission Statements are to be more detailed and precise.

All of the Mission Statements must directly support each of the Mission Statements that precede or follow. Mission

Statements are hierarchal which means that the flow proceeds from the top down. However, the implementation of the Mission Statement proceeds upwards from the individual level to the General Mission Statement.

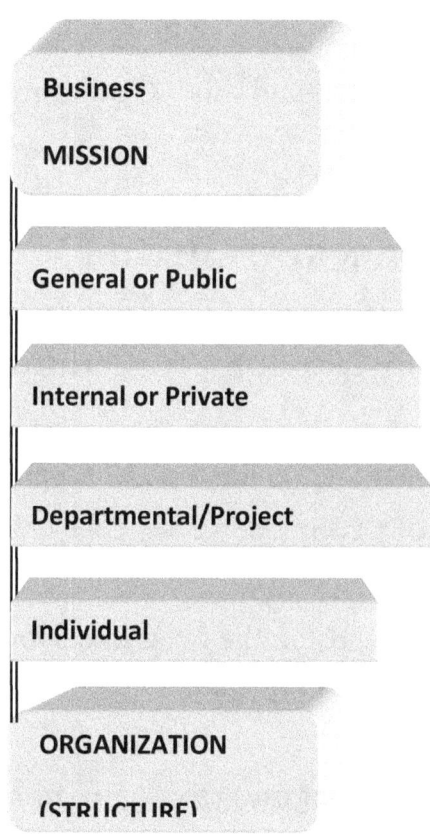

Illustration 3-1

MISSION STATEMENTS MODULE

The structure of the Organization must be formulated to meet the goals of the business, as delineated in the business's Mission Statements. The Mission Statements' Module, shown in

Illustration 3-1 depicts this direct link between the business's Mission Statements and its Organizational Structure.

EXAMPLES OF MISSION STATEMENTS:

EXTERNAL (Public): PROVIDE THE HIGHEST LEVEL OF SERVICE TO
EACH OF OUR CUSTOMERS, TO FACILITATE THEIR ACHIEVEMENT OF SUCCESS.

Comments: Wording depends on the types of customers and the product(s) and/or services provided.

INTERNAL: (Private): ACHIEVE MAXIMUM PROFIT FOR THE ENTERPRISE
WITHIN THE LEGAL, MORAL, AND ETHICAL GUIDELINES OF THE COMMUNITY, BEING EVER MINDFUL OF OUR ONGOING RESPONSIBILITIES TOWARDS OUR CUSTOMERS, EMPLOYEES, AND THE COMMUNITY AT LARGE.

Comments: It is ludicrous to act as if: For-Profit Companies are not in business to make money. Why don't the employees know this simple truth?

Non-Profit Organizations should identify performance and efficiency to maximize their service, etc., to their clients.

DEPARTMENTAL/PROJECT: PROVIDE THE NECESSARY LEADERSHIP, DIRECTION, AND LOGISTICAL SUPPORT TO ALL EMPLOYEES, ON A DAILY BASIS, TO ENABLE THEM TO MEET THEIR INDIVIDUALLY ASSIGNED TASKS.

INDIVIDUAL: REMAIN FOCUSED, AND TAKE ALL ACTION NECESSARY TO COMPLETE THE REQUIRED DAILY RESPONSIBILITIES COMMENSURATE WITH THE ASSIGNED LEVEL OF AUTHORITY AND RESPONSIBILITY.

Comments: Employees must have a full and complete understanding of their daily work assignments, be given the necessary resources, and authority to be successful, and held accountable for their performance. This is Management's responsibility

and is identified in the Departmental/Project Mission Statement.

———————

The only things that evolve by themselves in an organization are disorder, friction, and malperformance.
Peter F. Drucker[2] (1909-)

We trained hard, but it seemed that every time we were beginning to form up into teams, we would be reorganized. I was to learn later in life that we tend to meet any new situation by reorganizing, and a wonderful method it can be for creating the illusion of progress while producing confusion, inefficiency and demoralization.
Caius Petronius[3] 66 CE

The above quote of Caius Petronius refers not to changes required to maintain an organization's equilibrium in a dynamic environment, or to improve the performance of the organization in order to attain healthy growth and prosperity, but rather refers to changes made by an organization to obfuscate a marginal or deteriorating situation.

ORGANIZATION: *n,* **1. a group of people identified by shared interests**
   or purpose, for example a business.

3. the relationships that exist between separate elements arranged into a coherent whole.

STRUCTURE: *n,* **2. a system or organization made of interrelated parts**
   functioning as an orderly whole.

The foundation of any business is the organizational structure
   upon which the enterprise is built. Yet there is no aspect of a business that is more sorely neglected, over time, than the organizational structure. Limitations in a business's organizational structure will always result in reduced overall efficiency and performance of the business as a whole. **As a fundamental precept it would be accurate to state that a business can only be as good as its organizational structure allows.**

There are two distinct components to any organizational

structure: the Physical Structure, and the Personnel Structure i.e., more precisely the Personnel Function Organization.

While the importance of the Physical Structure cannot be overemphasized, it is beyond the scope of this book to cover all of the elements necessary to ensure the efficacy of the Physical Structure to fit the needs of the business. Suffice to say that the Physical Structure must meet the minimum requirements necessary to address the ongoing demands of the enterprise's Mission Statement. Illustration 3-2 is an example of simple Physical Structure Organization Chart. I have placed the FACILITY in the top position. However, for a retail business, as an example, LOCATION might logically be pre-eminent.

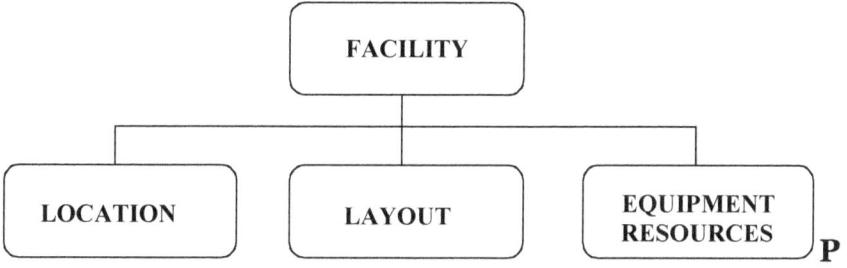

PHYSICAL STRUCTURE ORGANIZATION CHART

Illustration 3-2

Any inherent limitations that emerge from the Physical Structure, which cannot be remedied in the Physical Structure, must be addressed and compensated for in the Personnel Function Structure, and through the specific Policies and Guidelines of the business. It is of the utmost importance that the Physical Structure Organization and the Personnel Function Structure be mutually supportive.

If the only tool you have is a hammer, you tend to see
   every problem as a nail.
   Abraham H. Maslow[4] (1908-1970)

The Critical Zone Formula implies that the Personnel Structure must be kept as flat as feasible, and the Span of

Control must be limited based on functional responsibilities. There is the recent example of Organization Structural deficiencies and Span of Control problems in the Coalition Provisional Authority's unsatisfactory performance in Iraq immediately following the overthrow of the Saddam Regime. The book *FIASCO*[5] would be an interesting read for those desiring to learn about the disastrous consequences which can result from organizational hubris and the complete ignorance of basic management fundamentals in an organization comprised of the highly educated, woefully inexperienced, and entirely untrained. To think that similar experiences do not exist to some degree or other in many organizations and businesses around the world today would be delusional.

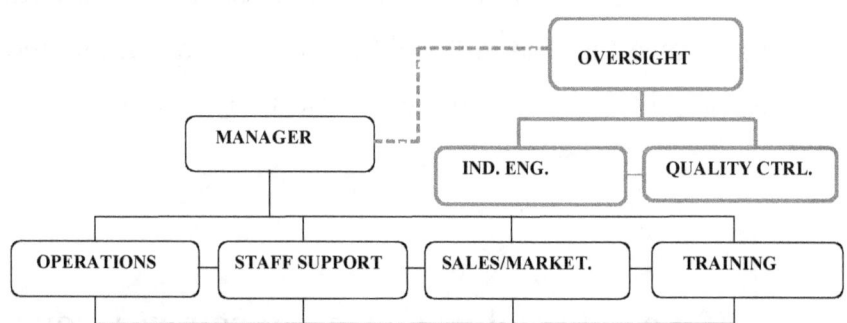

PERSONNEL FUNCTION ORGANIZATION CHART

Illustration 3-3

OPERATIONS: SALES OVERSIGHT

Product Engineering **Regional** **Ind. Engineering**
Mfg. Engineering **National** **Quality Control**
Production **International** **(Outside Auditors)**
Maintenance **Internet**
Material Control

STAFF SUPPORT: **TRAINING:**
Accounting **Administrative**
Human Resources **Operations**
Information Tech. **Technical**
Purchasing **Management**
Security **Sales/Marketing**

COMMENTS:

Illustration 3-3 is an example of a mature manufacturing operation's organization chart, (as opposed to a new or start-up business). Note: In this particular example, ***Production***, under the Operations Category, defines the Critical Zone. All other functions shown in the chart exist to support the Critical Zone. The interconnecting lines shown between each function on the chart indicate that the functions must be totally integrated in order to achieve the goals of the business as identified in the Mission Statements.

In this example, I have identified Accounting as a Staff Support function, which is appropriate for a manufacturing entity. Unfortunately, Accounting, is often placed in a position of ultimate authority in determining how a non-financial business, as opposed to a financial business, e.g., bank, investment company, venture capitalist, etc., is to be managed. Chapter Four will go into more detail on this pervasive problem. (Maslow's quote regarding the hammer, shown above has hit the nail right on the head. [Excuse the pun, if you must.])

The Personnel Organization Structure must be set-up to avoid inherent conflicts of interest. The OVERSIGHT section of the Personnel Chart establishes this pre-requisite. In this example, the OVERSIGHT function establishes an arm's length relationship between the Production Manager, the I.E. function, and the Q.C. function. The Production Manager has the responsibility to meet the daily production schedule. The I.E. function is to ensure that the established production processes and standard hours are maintained. The Q.C. function's primary purpose is to safeguard product quality. If the OVERSIGHT function did not exist, conflicts could arise in a situation where achieving the production schedule was considered more important than methods, standards and/or part quality.

The Audit function, an inherent function of the OVERSIGHT section, (which is often performed by an outside or independent agency), is established to ensure compliance of the Accounting Department, and the H.R

Department with all company policies, and all the legal requirements of federal, state, and local government agencies.

No matter how many branches, or levels are delineated in the Personnel Function Organization one person is in charge. In that one person, at the top position, resides the total authority, responsibility, and accountability for the success or failure of the organization as a whole. (Likewise, at each level of the organization the one person in charge of that level is totally responsible for the performance at that level.)

It should be obvious at this point, that a business's organization charts will have to be uniquely tailored to the nature of the business. Timely revisions to the organization will be necessary to keep abreast of the developments and expansions of the business.

Eagles don't flock. You have to find them one at a time.
Ross Perot[6], (1930-)

The reasonable man adapts himself to the world. The unreasonable man persists in trying to adapt the world to himself. Therefore all progress depends on the unreasonable man.

George Bernard Shaw[7], Man and Superman, (1903)

STAFFING: *tr.v.* **1. to provide with a staff of workers, or assistants.**

Businesses are made up of people interacting with people for the

purpose of conducting business with people. This fundamental and irrefutable fact seems to have little bearing on how businesses are run in today's world. Employees are often treated as the least valuable components of the business, followed closely by customers, and investors. The outlook for change in the near future is dim as long as Business As Usual is the predominant viewpoint of the business community. **PAY ATTENTION PLEASE! BUSINESS IS ALL ABOUT PEOPLE. EVERYTHING ELSE IS SECONDARY.**

Jim Collins' book: *Good to Great:*[8], addresses, amongst other areas, the importance of hiring the right people for the business, positioning the right people within the organization, removing the wrong people from the organization, (when it has been carefully determined that they do not fit in the organization), and retaining the right people. It is of utmost importance that the correct number of people required to accomplish the goals of the business also be in place.

We hire credentials and fire personalities. I read this statement in a newspaper article in the business section of the local newspaper. What are we to look for in hiring? Education, both formal and informal, is important. Experience is important. Energy and motivation are important. Honesty and integrity are important. An individual can have all these important attributes and because of his/her personality be entirely unsuited for a position in a particular business or company. Personality is the most important of all the determinants to be considered when staffing. Remember that a business is also a culture, i.e., A particular set of attitudes that characterizes a group of people. To realize success over the long term, there must be general harmony within the culture, which can be achieved only through common focus, and dedication to achieving the goals of the organization.

Hiring people based primarily on credentials is comparatively simple. Verify the authenticity of the credentials and your main criteria for employment qualification has been achieved. While it is absolutely necessary to verify the credentials of all candidates, a great deal of skill, effort, and time is required to ascertain the personality of a candidate. (Refer to Chapter One.)

The skill, motivation, and experience of the interviewers

will determine whether or not the interview will yield a successful candidate. The interviewers all must be well trained. The interview sessions must be carefully planned and adhere to established formal procedures as regards methodology and evaluation.

The Human Resources Department has a significant and important role to play in verifying the candidate's credentials, ensuring compliance with all government regulations, and administering qualification tests, as the company deems appropriate. The HR Department must properly present the company's policies and benefits package to the prospective employee. However, unless the candidate is interviewing for a position within the HR Department, the HR Department, lacking the requisite qualifications and experience, should not have the deciding vote in the hiring of a candidate, (assuming all other prerequisites are met), for a position outside of the HR Department. There is a trend in business today wherein such responsibility and authority in the hiring process is granted to the Human Resource Department. Unfortunate consequences often result.

The problem with the whole process of interviewing job candidates is that an interview is often viewed as an additional task tacked on to the daily activities of the people appointed to perform the interview. As such, the interview then becomes something of a distraction that must be speedily, and often grudgingly, concluded. (This is one of the reasons that this essential charge is often foisted upon the Human Resources department.)

The interviewer must be knowledgeable, motivated, focused on the critical importance of the interview process, and well trained in order to be successful in this undertaking. Great companies never lose sight of the value and importance of their employees at all levels. Great companies are willing to spend the time, money, and effort required to ensure that they continue to remain great. A formula for success: Great People = Great Companies = Continued Success.

_____

Make Haste Slowly!
Caesar Augustus[9] (63 BCE-14 CE)

GROWTH: n, 1. the process of becoming larger and more mature through
   natural development.
   2. an increase in numbers, size, power, or intensity.

CHANGE: v, 1. to cause to be different.

TRANSITION: n, 1. a process or period in which something undergoes a change and passes from one

state, stage, form, or activity to another.

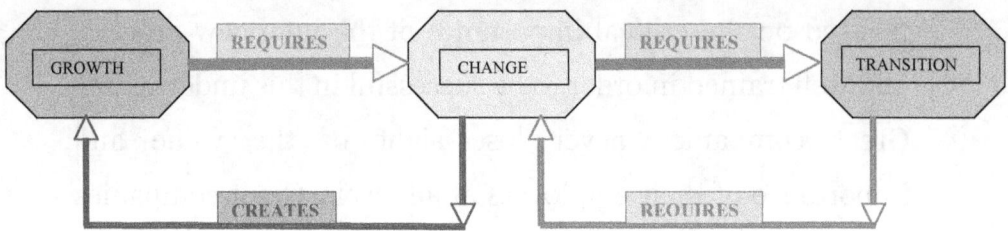

Illustration 3-4

Illustration 3-4 depicts the two cyclic processes related to growth in businesses. The Law of Entropy is always in force, so there is ongoing change. However, since entropic change always leads to disorder, the CHANGE shown above must be positive in form in order for GROWTH to be realized. Continued GROWTH requires continuous positive change. However, CHANGE imposed just does not work. CHANGE, which is situational, requires TRANSITION, which is psychological[10]. Given that CHANGE is constant, either positive or negative, TRANSITION, then, is also constant and will always be in the same direction as CHANGE. Businesses cannot successfully effect the positive CHANGE required for sustained GROWTH unless they successfully manage TRANSITION. TRANSITION is always a people challenge!

In order to stay in business, a business must achieve

sustained growth. For example, the annualized inflation rate in the United States from 1956-2006 was 4.09%. As the result of this inflation it would require $7.42 in 2006, to equal the buying power of $1.00 in 1956.[11] There are numerous factors other than inflation driving the need for growth. However, those considerations are outside the scope of this book. Suffice to say, continuous growth is mandatory for survival

The operative word in the definition of growth, shown above, is <u>process</u>. Ignoring the reality of said universal laws, Wall Street's seeming emphasis on growth and short-term profitability can be very detrimental to the success and well being of any business whose management does not understand or comply with all of the conditions that must be met in the short term, in order to achieve success for their business in the long term. There are those who would have us believe that faster, and bigger are better. Time, as with any resource, is an asset only when properly managed. Bigger: Are bureaucracies better; are conglomerates better? The appropriate question to ask here is, Better for whom?

The Growth-Change-Transition process is controlled by the Universal Laws governing systems. (Refer to Chapter Two). Entropy, as stated above, is ever-present. The Pareto Principle and Parkinson's Laws are applicable in every situation and at all times. Monitoring, evaluating, and directing the Growth-Change-Transition process is a critical

Management responsibility upon which depends the long-term survival of the business. The Transition Process will require the most effort. Long-term success can only be achieved if the employees have all been well chosen.

SUMMARY:

Mission Statements are extremely important, for they not only define the goals, but also the culture of a business.

Each business must have a general External Mission Statement and several, more precise, Internal Mission Statements.

The Organizational Structure of a business is directly linked to the
Mission Statements.

The Organizational Structure has two Components: Physical and
Personnel.

Limitations in the Physical Organizational Structure must be addressed and compensated for in the Personnel Organization Structure, and through specific policies and guidelines.

Rule of Staffing: Hire on the basis of Personality, then credentials.

To achieve success, a business must: hire the right people; hire the right number of people to accomplish the mission; position the right people where they can be successful in the organization; carefully weed out the people who cannot fit in the organization; and retain the right people.

A business must have sustained growth in order to survive.

Sustained growth is the product of a cyclic process involving positive change and effective transition.

The universal laws governing systems control the Growth-Change-Transition process.

Transition is a people challenge.

Management has a prime responsibility for monitoring, evaluating, and directing the Growth-Change-Transition process.

Chapter Four
Management & Focus

Responsibility is a unique concept: it can only reside and inhere in a single individual. You may share it with others, but your portion is not diminished. You may delegate it, but it is still with you. You may disclaim it, but you cannot divest yourself of it. Even if you do not recognize it or admit its presence, you cannot escape it. If responsibility is rightfully yours, no evasion, or ignorance, or passing blame can shift the burden to someone else. Unless you can point your finger at the man who is responsible when something goes wrong, then you have never held/had anyone really responsible.
Hyman G. Rickover[1] (1900-1986)

AUTHORITY: *n.* **3.** power to act on behalf of somebody else or official permission to do so.

RESPONSIBILITY: *n.* **1. the state, fact, or position of being accountable to somebody or for something.**

CONSEQUENCE: *n.* **1. something that follows as a result.**

1 2 3

Illustration: 4-1

Illustration: 4-2

Illustration 4-1 depicts a critical process, which is much misunderstood and/or ignored in business these days. (Although responsibility and accountability are considered to be synonyms, I have included both words in the illustration to emphasize that accountability is an inherent part of responsibility.)

Illustration 4-2 uses the three legged stool analogy to represent the Authority-Responsibility-Consequences in a different manner. This illustration emphasizes the importance of all three elements in the management process being integrated, and functioning properly in order to ensure ongoing success in accomplishing the mission. It is obvious that if one of the legs of the stool is broken or missing, the business, like the stool, falls over.

There are a number of common problems associated with the breakdown of the Authority-Responsibility-Consequences Process: Abuse of authority; disregard of proper authority; assignment of responsibility without commensurate authority; responsibility without consequences etc. There is a long list of such perturbations. Why do these problems, which cause so much disruption to good order in the workplace happen? These problems happen because employees are uninformed, untrained, un-accountable, and un-audited, by the people placed in authority above them. Ignorance of basic management fundamentals is the root cause of the problems.

The beginning of wisdom is the ability to call things by their right names.
Confucius[2] (551-479 BCE)

MANAGER: *n.* **1. somebody who is responsible for directing and controlling the work and personnel of a business, or of a particular department within a business.**

MANAGEMENT: *n.* **1. the organizing and controlling of the affairs of a business or a particular sector of a business.**

Hopefully, by now, we can begin to see the critical importance of having effective management in a business enterprise. It is worth emphasizing that the function of management requires more than a title assigned to a person whose primary responsibilities lie elsewhere, e.g., sales, accounting, engineering, etc. The management function is in itself the primary responsibility of the person employed in a management position, be it the head of a team, department, division, or company. This brings up another point: Let's get back to calling the position "Manager". Simple and accurate is better than clever and inaccurate. Imprecision of description over time leads to deterioration of that which is being described. The dictionary definitions of "manager" and "management" quoted above are clear and concise: Organize, direct, and control the affairs of the business.

The essential qualifications necessary for a successful manager are in order of priority: People Skills, Communication Skills, Technical Competence, Education, and Training Expertise. The higher the management level, the higher the qualifications required in all of these areas. There is another factor that separates the effective from the ineffective manager: Love of the challenge that the position of Manager engenders. If you don't love being in management, you will never excel at management.

I read a statement written in a book on management, which said in summary, that with the advent of current technology in the information age, employees now have become self-empowered, and therefore the position of management has become obsolete. I would say rather that understanding the proper role of management has become obsolete. The marginalization of the management function has led us to where we are in the marketplace today: too many businesses operating at an unsatisfactory level of performance.

On the other hand, micromanagement, also common in the workplace today, is the antithesis of effective management. If the employees are competent to perform the tasks for which they were hired, the task of the manager is to guide these employees using loose reins, and not choking them. Micromanagers are not qualified to be managers in the first place for they operate on the basis of their own personal fears, which in turn will always contaminate the work environment. Micromanagement is a destroyer of employee initiative, creativity, loyalty, and morale.

Effective managers share a common trait: the desire to be of service. (Service goes both up and down the organization's hierarchal ladder.) Successful managers <u>lead</u> by example. Ralph Waldo Emerson[3], the great American Poet said: "Who you are speaks so loudly I can't hear what you are saying." There is a common misunderstanding prevalent in business today that there is a distinct difference between a manager and a leader. This is an error which arises from the misconception about the role of the management function and the personal qualifications required to be an effective manager.

The manager is required to ensure that all of his/her employees are provided with the total resources necessary to perform their individual work scope. These resources would include: guidance and direction, time, equipment, materials, and training. (Until the manager has fulfilled his/her obligation to supply all of the necessary resources, the employees cannot be held accountable for any lack of performance resulting from insufficiency of such resources.)

In addition to their role as service provider, managers are responsible for the resolution of conflicts arising each day when valid operational demands exceed the limited resources available. Carrying out the day-to-day mission of the business then is properly left to the employees.

Beyond the daily service requirements to his/her employees, the manager is responsible for personnel safety, intermediate and long-term planning, scheduling, budget development, cost control, training, growth, modernization, community relations, and community involvement.

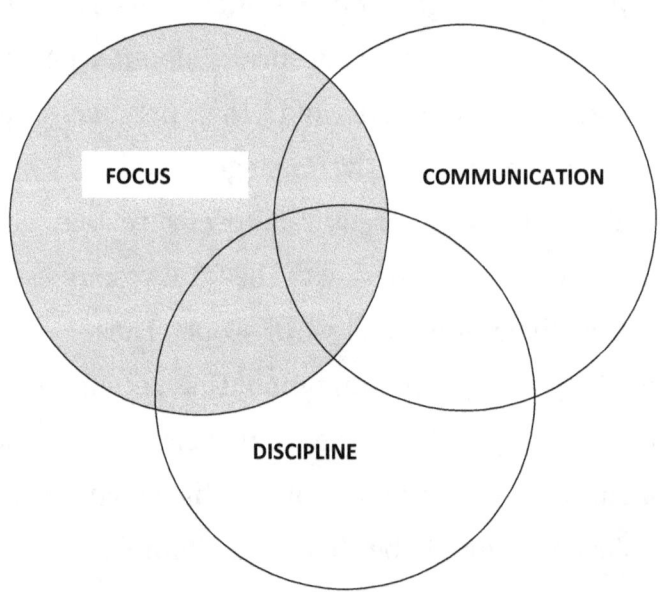

Illustration 4-3

FOCUS: *n.* 1. concentrated effort or attention on a particular thing

CONCENTRATE: *v.* 2. to direct attention, time, and resources to one particular area or activity, usually over a period of time.

PERFORMANCE: *n.* 3. the effectiveness of the way somebody does his/her job.

This piece is not about multi-tasking per se, (see Chapter One), although the information presented applies. Rather the emphasis here is on lack of focus, which occurs whenever an individual is performing one task <u>while thinking about something else</u>. Take a simple example: I am driving my car to work and while driving I am thinking about what I am going to do when I get there. A straightforward mathematical formula illustrates the effect on performance efficiency from any such a loss of focus.

Formula: OPE=C/N
where: **OPE=Overall Performance Efficiency in Percent(%)**
C=Concentration. C is a constant equal to 1.
N=Number of elements in progress at one moment in time.

Examples: OPE=C/N where C=1 and N=1; where C=1 and N=2

OPE=1/1 OPE=1/2

<u>OPE=100%</u> <u>OPE=50%</u>

Simply stated: **Optimum performance efficiency in accomplishing any task occurs only when the individual focuses on the task at hand, i.e., the individual's mind is concentrating on the action being undertaken.** Simple: Yes, difficult: Yes, impossible: NO! Specific training is required to develop the necessary awareness and self-discipline required for the individual employee to effectively overcome this problem of lack of focus (Training is covered in Chapter Six).

Anyone can do any amount of work provided it isn't
the work he is supposed to do at the moment.
Robert Benchley[4] (1889-1945)

JOB: *n.* 1 a regular activity performed in exchange for payment,
especially as one's trade, occupation, or profession.

PARAMETER: *n.* **1 a fact or circumstance that restricts how something**
  is done or what can be done.

As a manager, if I were to ask any supervisory or salary employee in my area of responsibility what their job was, they would tell me instead, some of the things they did. I came to realize over time that most employees were never given a precise description of their job specifics, i.e., job parameters. This is a very inefficient way to run a business, as the 80 **20** rule example will demonstrate. Keep in mind that Entropy and Parkinson's Law are also in play at all times.

A brief comment regarding Pareto's Principle is in order. This is a principle, which generally applies in most circumstances. The percentage split may vary either way, but for purposes of this presentation we will use **80 20**. Pareto's Principle applies to all aspects of the business: people, time, work elements, resources, etc.

Looking at it simply, the Pareto Principle identifies that 80% of an employees potential work effort will be expended on 20% of the work elements he/she encounter in the course of the day. This leaves 20% of the employees potential work effort to deal with the remaining 80% of the work elements. (I classify the 20% in this example as the "non-routine" and the 80% as the "routine".) Since the manager cannot know with absolute certainty what the non-routine unknowns are, he/she can only define the 80% routine work elements in the job work scope assigned to each employee. Failure to properly define the routine work elements for each employee results in the inefficiencies commonly found in the workplace today.

EXAMPLE: The Pareto Principle: Employees' output.
Team/Group Routine work = 100%

1st 20% of the employees accomplish 80% of the total = 80.0%

2nd 20% of the employees accomplish 80% of the 20% remaining = 16.0%

3rd 20% of the employees accomplish 80% of the 04% remaining = 03.2%

99.2%

The remaining 40% of the employees accomplish less than 01.0%

of the routine work.

The employees are all very busy doing something, (Parkinson's Law), and likely believe that they are working hard at what they should be doing. The obvious question then is what is being accomplished; what is the efficiency of output? The problem fallout as presented in this example will be manifest in numerous ways: staffing problems, duplication of effort, lack of adherence to procedures, missed opportunities, missed schedules, idle time, personal business, etc. You may think that the above is an extreme example and not relevant to the workplace today. Just look around and pay attention! The result of your careful observations and analysis might surprise you.

When the manager outlines the job parameters for an individual employee, he/she is also defining the employee's positional responsibilities. In other words, this definition identifies in general what the employee is required to do, and what the employee is prohibited from doing, (unless permission is received from their immediate supervisor). The manager has the additional responsibility to protect the employee from the intrusions of well-meaning people who have a better idea of what the employee should be doing than the employee. (The uncontrolled and undisciplined use of e-mail in the workplace today has all but destroyed the concept of the chain-of-command. E-mail will be covered in detail in Chapter Five.) The manager has the responsibility to create and maintain the work environment in such a manner that facilitates the employees' ability to remain focused on their work. Generally this is not an onerous or burdensome task for the manager if the "right" employees are correctly placed in their positions, and provided with all the resources they require to succeed at their jobs.

Employee job definition entails specific identification of the Authority-Responsibility-Consequences inherent in the position, which includes the company Mission Statements, organizational structure, chain of command, and reporting requirements. Other prerequisites involve: training, familiarization with company history, company goals and objectives, policies, standard procedures, and operational guidelines.

Company policies and procedures are specific and detailed written instructions, which define methodology, and are intended to ensure employee compliance with established company intent and standards. Operational guidelines, on the other hand, are not detailed and serve rather to point the direction in which the employee is to proceed in accomplishing their mission.

To be effective a manager must be a good leader. Conversely, a good leader must be an effective manager.

SUMMARY:

Inability to understand and control the Authority-Responsibility-Consequence process is a root cause of failure to achieve success in business.

"Manager" is not just a title. The position of manager is a critical full time occupation.

Successful managers must possess excellent: People Skills, Communication Skills, Technical Competence, Education, and Training Expertise.

A manager's role is to be of service to his superiors and his employees.

The manager controls the work environment.

Optimum performance efficiency occurs only when an individual focuses on the task at hand.

The Pareto Principle is operative in all aspects of a business: people, time, work elements, resources, etc. Entropy, and Parkinson's Law are also at play. The manager's job is to manage and control, positively, the effects of these universal laws operative in the workplace.

The manager defines the employees' work scope and level of authority and responsibility.

Company policies, procedures, and guidelines are established to define an employee's obligations and direction in the performance of their duties.

An effective manager is a leader who leads by example.

Chapter Five
Communication

It seemed rather incongruous that in a society of supersophisticated communication, we often suffer from a shortage of listeners.
 Erma Bombeck[1] (1927-1996)

COMMUNICATE: *v.* 2 to transmit or reveal a feeling or thought by speech, writing, or gesture, so that it is clearly understood.

HEAR: *v.* 4 to understand fully by listening attentively

LISTEN: *v.* 2 to pay attention to something and to take it into account.

OBSERVE: *v.* 1 to see or notice something, especially while watching carefully.

SPEAK: *v.* **2 to communicate thoughts, opinions, or feelings by uttering with the voice.**

In order for communication to be truly effective, all of the individual participants involved must be fully engaged at all times and at all levels, as depicted in Illustration 5-2.

**REQUIRES
COMMUNICATION**

**SUBCONSCIOUS
CONSCIOUS LEVEL MODULE LEVEL MODULE**

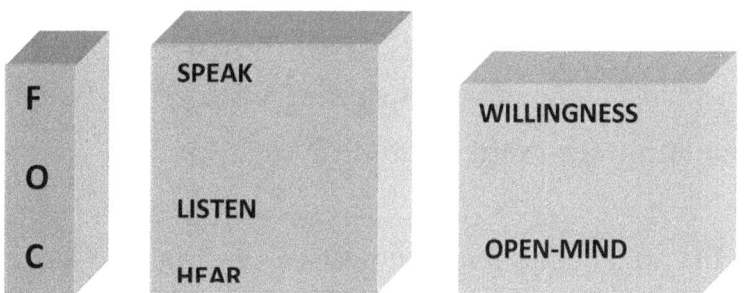

Illustration 5-2

To SPEAK, LISTEN-HEAR, are the obvious components of communication. Not so OBSERVE, which along with FOCUS, is critical to achieving effective communications. Perhaps a story from long ago, (source unknown to the author), will illustrate this important point.

Married Man: My wife and I don't seem to be able to get along anymore and the situation appears to be getting worse.

Marriage Counselor: For the next two weeks I want you to return home and listen very carefully to every word your wife speaks.

Two Weeks Later:

Married Man: I did as you instructed. I listened to every word my wife spoke. Things seem to be going a little better around the house.

Marriage Counselor: Excellent! Now I want you go home and for the next two weeks I want you to listen very carefully to every word your wife doesn't speak.

In order for communication to take place, the participants must be physically present. (Whether or not video conferencing, if properly done, will suffice to meet this specific requirement is doubtful but still open to conjecture.) This brings up a salient point: it is not possible to communicate in the true sense of the word using phones, radios, letters, or e-mails. These instruments can be used only to transmit and/or exchange information and data, not communicate.

The conscious level activities are interactive. The subconscious level elements are all individual and personal. The conscious level elements by themselves will not ensure successful communication unless the three elements identified in the subconscious level module are supportive. For example, if a person is not willing to listen, or does not have an open mind, or cannot accept a position different than their own, effective communication is not possible. *Communication can only be achieved when there is a mutual exchange of facts, ideas, opinions, and possibly feelings such that each participant is in agreement as to the <u>content</u> of the exchange.*

TYPICAL COMMUNICATION PROBLEMS:

Unfortunately, there is an increasing tendency in our culture to voice opinions rather than factual information when discussing problems, or differences. Opinions are fine, but unless there is factual information to back up the opinions, there is no credibility, and no possible progress to be gained towards resolution or agreement. Any disagreements that arise in a discussion should ultimately be resolved on the basis of factual information, not emotions or opinions.

Another communication problem which I call the "incomplete picture problem" occurs when a request is submitted for some action and no alternatives are presented.

For example, I request a piece of equipment, such as a pump costing several thousand dollars, to replace an aging pump having frequent mechanical breakdowns. I submit the request, which identifies the replacement pump costs, to the cognizant authority. However, unless I include the probable projected costs which could result from the total failure of the existing pump, I have not presented sufficient information for the cognizant authority to make a meaningful decision.

The English Language lends itself to precision if properly used. The problem is that the English language is not properly used by many, including people in positions of prominence who are the supposed examples the public may look to for guidance or emulation.

In business, precise use of language is paramount. For example, the use of adjectives such as good, bad, poor, etc. in describing conditions, situations, or events is neither precise nor is it factual. In the diversity of the global economy, cultural mores render such labels as subjective only, and therefore these types of words should not be used in support of a position taken in any discussion.

Illogical thinking is another area of difficulty frequently encountered in communication. If the participants have not been taught to think and speak simply, clearly, and logically, all kinds of nonsense can emerge from a discussion because the proposal or solution sounds "good" or seems to make sense when, in fact it is not logically based. To paraphrase an old computer slogan: Nonsense in....nonsense out!

Assumptions are never helpful and often lead to misunderstanding! However, if assumptions must be made, all the participants must know that the information shared was based on an assumption with a clear identification of that assumption.

The Computer is a moron.
Peter F. Drucker[2] (1909-)

ELECTRONIC MAIL, i.e., e-mail *n* **1 a system for transmitting messages and data from one computer to another.**

PROTOCOL: *n.* **2 the rules of correct or appropriate behavior for a particular group of people, or in a particular situation.**

Unstructured and undisciplined use of e-mail within businesses likely arose with the introduction of e-mail ahead of the protocol required to properly administer and control its use internally.

E-mail is an essential tool for transmitting data and information and documenting such transmissions for record keeping purposes. In order for e-mail to be an effective tool, its use in the workplace must be controlled. Without going into specific detail, the protocol for use of e-mail in the business should address the following categories:

- DEFINITION OF PURPOSE
- CHAIN OF COMMAND
  - INTERNAL
  - EXTERNAL
- CONTENT DESCRIPTION
- RECORD KEEPING
- REVIEW FREQUENCY
- AUDIT PROCEDURES
- TRAINING

Remember: e-mail is not a substitute for communication. Any individual holding a management position who routinely uses e-mail to direct his/her employees, instead of dealing with them in person, simply does not belong in management.

INTERNET: *n.* **a network that links computer networks all over the world by satellite and telephone connecting users with service networks**

The internet is an indispensable tool required for business. However, there is a major problem of lost productivity existent in business today associated with employees' unsanctioned personal use of the internet during working hours. Trying to control and treat this problem only by strict enforcement of company policies is treating the consequence (symptom) instead of addressing the root cause of the problem. Consider this: If the business has properly focused and motivated employees, each having a well-defined and practical work-scope, being led by a supportive manager, and working hard to achieve the company's mission, the problems of employees' misuse of the internet will be minimal or non-existent.

_____

INFORMATION TECHNOLOGY:

This section addresses the Information Technology (**IT**) Department as a support function within a business organization rather than the Information Technology Industry.

We are in the midst of an information technology revolution. Unfortunately, there seems to be a mindset in some IT Departments, that their department exists for its own sake. IT Departments exist to support the mission statements of the business. Failure to support the goals and objectives of all the departments within the business is a disservice to the business. There are a number of self-generated fallacies that have contributed to this unfortunate attitude within the IT Department Hierarchy. Some examples are as follows:

The company must have the latest in hardware and software in order to: become competitive, remain competitive, or lead the competition, i.e., "Newer is Better!"

The new software program will meet 100% of all requirements.

The new software program has additional modules which can be added to the system as needed for future expansion.

The new system will be installed according to our schedule with no interruptions to operations.

System Maintenance takes precedence over operational requirements.

The task of management is to pay heed to the valid recommendations of the IT Department relating to the acquisition of new technology. However, management must always evaluate the timing and acquisition of such technology to ensure that the best interests of the business are protected. Additionally, management has the ongoing task to ensure that all departments, including the IT Department are mutually supportive and working towards achieving the mission of the business at all times.

The IT Department has the responsibility to establish a written protocol for each document that accompanies the release of operational software to be used in the business. The protocol should cover in specific detail the following elements:

- The Primary purpose of the document
- The Secondary purpose(s) of the document
- The Owner of the document, i.e., the individual responsible for control of the document
- Primary users
- Secondary users
- Document Routing
- Integration of the document with existing, new, or modified documents
- Document audit requirements and frequency of audits
- Management oversight identification

SUMMARY:

Communication requires the following: physical presence, focus, conscious and unconscious elements, and agreement by all participants as to the content of the exchange.

Phones, radios, letters, or e-mails can only transmit and or/exchange information/data.

The English language lends itself to precision if properly used. Precision is absolutely required in business at all times.

Typical communication problems: Opinions instead of facts; incomplete information; illogical thinking and presentation; unidentified assumptions.

E-mail is an essential and effective tool if properly utilized. A detailed e-mail protocol is required to control its use.

Proper attitude and employee motivation will minimize or preclude misuse of the internet.

The business community is in the midst of an information technology revolution.

The Information Technology Department's primary purpose is to support the mission of the business.

Management must exercise prudent judgment when making the decision as to whether or not to acquire new information technology.

The IT Department is responsible for initiation and control of documents for use within the company. Management is responsible for the oversight of document release and use.

Chapter Six
Discipline

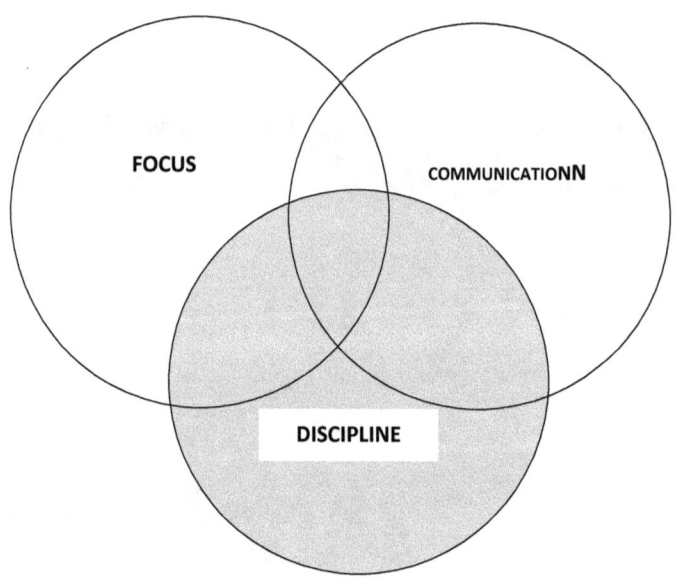

Illustration 6-1

There is no discipline in the world so severe as the discipline of experience subjected to the tests of intelligent development and direction.
John Dewey[1] (1859-1952)

Greatness is more than potential. It is the execution of that potential. Beyond the raw talent you need the appropriate training. You need the discipline. You need the inspiration. You need the drive.
Eric A. Burns[2] (1968-)

DISCIPLINE: *n.* **1. training expected to produce a specific or pattern of behavior.**

TRAINING: *n.* **1. the process of teaching or learning a skill or job.**

(Note: It may be helpful to review Chapter One before proceeding on with this chapter**)**

Failure to provide proper training to employees at every phase and at every level is not only a great disservice to the employees themselves; it is a great disservice to the business, the customers, the owners, and the community at large. Untrained employees cannot be properly motivated, creative, productive, or efficient. In the long run the business cannot be successful.

Training requires a competent Trainer, a willing and trainable Trainee, and the appropriate Training Programs. Training responsibility resides in a number of departments within the business.

Consideration must be given by businesses to provide remedial training in reading comprehension and basic mathematics to entrance level employees in localities where there is an insufficient number of otherwise qualified candidates available for work. (This would require an additional Training Module, not shown, and is beyond the scope of this book.)

If possible, Management should encourage their employees to continue their formal education in their respective fields, through company financial incentives.

Training Modules

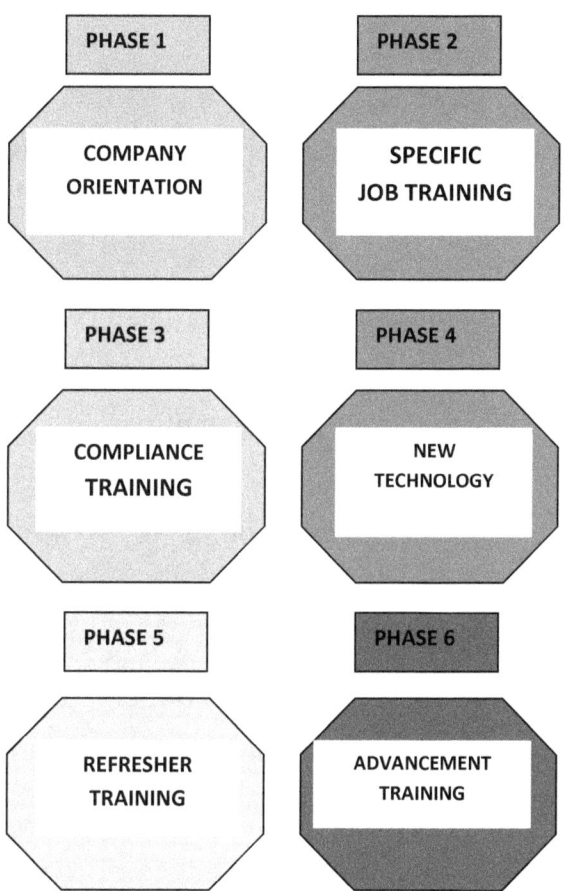

Illustration 6-2

General:

Each Department/Section/Team, i.e., Unit, should have an assigned Training Coordinator responsible for overseeing all training in his/her area of responsibility.

Each Training Module requires a specific, written training protocol, including a training element check-off sheet.

Management has the responsibility to make certain that training at all levels and in all phases is a matter of company policy that is routinely accomplished as required.

Management has the responsibility to ensure that *Outsourced*
Training Packages are relevant to operational requirements, and verify that the Trainers have the appropriate background and experience necessary to properly train their employees.

Employees have the responsibility to accept all company training as a job-requirement, and put forth the commensurate effort required to be successful. This applies whether the training is conducted on-site or off-site.

Phase 1 - COMPANY ORIENTATION TRAINING:

Responsibility: Human Resources

Training Elements:

Company History: Origins to Present

Mission Statements

Regulations, Policies, Guidelines

Internet/e-mail Protocol

Company Staff

Organization Charts

Community Involvement

Safety - General, e.g., Evacuation Plans

Employee's Training Program and Schedule

Employee's Performance Evaluation Schedule

Phase 2 - SPECIFIC JOB TRAINING:

Responsibility: Assigned Unit Training Coordinator

Training Elements:

Department/Section Staff

Organization Charts

Unit e-mail Protocol

Employee's Work Scope Assignment

Safety - Job Specific

"Progression of Learning" Schedule

Employee's Performance Milestones

Employee's Evaluation Process

Phase 3 - COMPLIANCE TRAINING

Responsibility: Human Resources, Assigned Unit Training Coordinator, Outside Agencies

Phase 3 - COMPLIANCE TRAINING, (Cont.):

Training Elements: As Required

Examples: EPA; OSHA, Federal, State, and County Laws,

Financial Regulations, ISO 9000, etc.

Phase 4 - NEW TECHNOLOGY TRAINING:

Responsibility: Human Resources, Assigned Unit Training Coordinator, Outside Agencies

Training Elements: As Required

Examples: New computer software/hardware, new machinery,

etc.

Phase 5 - REFRESHER TRAINING:

Responsibility: Human Resources, Assigned Unit Training Coordinator, Outside Agencies

Training Elements:

Phase 1, 2 Modules; Phase 3: Recertification as required

Phase 6 - ADVANCEMENT TRAINING:

Responsibility: Human Resources, Assigned Unit Training
    Coordinator, Outside Agencies

Training Elements:

Phase 2, 3 Modules, and As Required

Examples: Technical Advancement, Advancement in Grade
    Promotion to Management, Management Advancement, etc.

———————

Thousands of officers in all of our services knew John Boyd by his work on what was to be known as the Boyd Cycle or OODA Loop. His writings and his lectures had a fundamental impact on the curriculum of virtually every professional military program in the United States----and on many abroad. In this way, he touched so many lives, many of them destined to ascend to the highest levels of military and civilian leadership.

C.C. Krulak[3] (1942-)

OODA LOOP SKETCH

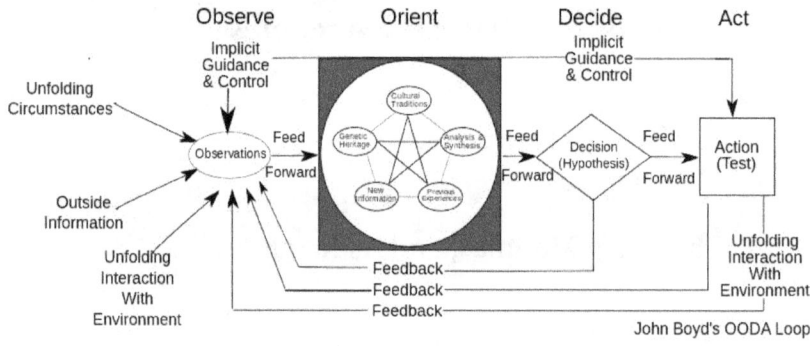

Illustration 6-3[4]

JOHN R. BOYD'S OODA LOOP:

Colonel Boyd, USAF, was an innovative and creative thinker whose ideas, many believe, revolutionized modern warfare. Additionally, the OODA LOOP: OBSERVE-ORIENT-DECIDE-ACT has gained recognition in the business world as a viable and useful management tool. The book *CERTAIN TO WIN, by* Chet Richards[5] demonstrates the application of John Boyd's Strategy to business. This book should be considered as a recommended read for every management and prospective management employee.

After due consideration, I decided that since the OODA Loop was probably unknown to most people, and since I felt strongly that the concept and application of the OODA LOOP should be a part of the specific job training for all management, marketing, and sales personnel, (at a minimum), the presentation rightly belonged in the Chapter on DISCIPLINE. A detailed analysis of the OODA LOOP is beyond the scope of this book. However, there is a great deal of information on John Boyd's Ideas and Presentations available in various publications and on the Internet.

To add to my comments on OBSERVATION in CHAPTER ONE, (ref. The OODA LOOP), everyone and collectively every organization has an OODA LOOP. If the challenge of the OODA LOOP is to react inside the response time, i.e., faster than the response time of my competition, then it is imperative for me not only to know the truth about myself, but to the degree possible, know the truth about the person or organization that I am dealing with.

According to the OODA LOOP, we observe events through the filter of the ORIENT module. The ORIENT module consists of a number of imprinted programs in our mind, i.e., Cultural Traditions, Genetic Heritage, and

Previous Experience, which will determine how an individual will interpret and process new information flowing into the ORIENT module from the OBSERVE module. However, usage of the OODA LOOP requires detailed analysis of oneself, the organization to which one belongs, and knowledge of the other person/organization before a decision on a course of action is made and implemented. Lacking either one of these two elements renders the OODA LOOP ineffective. Individual self-introspection is mandatory and the ability to think logically, and analyze the competition is essential in order to be able to utilize and benefit from using tools such as the OODA Loop.

Cultural traditions and genetic heritage play a central role in the orientation perspective. Unfortunately, in the United States today, we as a society are for the most part culturally ignorant, not only of our own culture, but of the cultures of the world. How then do we expect to compete and prosper in the Global Economy? Our public education system needs a massive overhaul. "No child left behind". How about: "Don't leave our Country behind?" To overcome the deficiencies of the public educational system, businesses will have to play an increasing role in the education of their workforce, and undertake the required training of their employees, at all levels. This requirement will have an increasing priority in the immediate future. Our current deficiencies in education and training cannot be allowed to continue if we are to achieve long-term success in the Global Economy.

SUMMARY:

Failure to properly train employees is a major error on the part of businesses and will ultimately lead to long-term deleterious consequences for those businesses that do not train their employees.

Training requires a competent trainer, a willing and trainable trainee, and the appropriate training programs.

Each business unit must have assigned training coordinators responsible for overseeing all training within their unit.

There are six Training Modules covering the training required for business organizations.

Each Training Module requires a specific written training protocol.

Management is required to oversee and enforce all training within the business.

Employees have the responsibility to accept all company training as a job-requirement, and perform accordingly.

John R. Boyd's OODA LOOP is an essential training tool for business in today's global economy.

OODA LOOP Training should be mandatory for all management, sales, and marketing personnel, as a minimum.

Business will be forced to undertake the training and become more deeply involved in the education of the workforce in order to remain competitive in the global economy.

Chapter Seven
Conclusion

The essence of optimism is that it takes no account of the present, but it is a source of inspiration, of vitality and hope where others have resigned; it enables a man to hold his head high, to claim the future for himself and not to abandon it to his enemy.
Dietrich Bonhoeffer[1] (1906-1945)

SCIENTIFIC: *n.* 1 the study of the physical world and its manifestations, especially by using systematic observations and experiment

UNIVERSAL: *adj.* 1 affecting, relating to, including the whole world or everyone in the world

COMMENTARY:

Generally, businesses are not operated on the basis of universal scientific principles. The question then is, why not?

Let us look briefly at the three universal principles that were presented in Chapter Two: *Entropy,* the *Pareto Principle,* and *Parkinson's Law.*

ENTROPY:

Austrian Physicist Ludwig Eduard Boltzman developed the mathematical equation for entropy: *S=k log W*, between 1872-1875. The development of entropy in the industrial revolution lead to the field of thermodynamics, the branch of physics dealing with the conversion of various forms of energy. "The tendency of physical systems to evolve towards states of entropy is known as the 2nd Law of Thermodynamics."[2] Entropy is often applied to other situations, such as the complexity of life, or orderliness."[3] Can this concept be extrapolated to other areas outside of the realm of physics? There is scientific disagreement on this issue! However, I would ask the reader to make their own observations of any organization over time, and come to their own conclusions. My lifelong scrutiny of organizations supports the dictionary definition used earlier in Chapter Two, i.e., Entropy is the "inevitable and steady deterioration of a system or society".

The disagreement, which sometimes exists between scientists and the non-scientific community, may explain why organizations, including businesses, have not felt it necessary to seek out and apply universal principles to their own specific enterprises.

Additionally, there exists the problem of dissemination of information of scientific discoveries relating to universal principles from within the realm of pure science to the general public. Scientists continue to evaluate, modify, and/or eliminate their theories based on experimentation and new information. Over time, others outside of the pure scientific realm begin to explore these theories and discoveries and postulate the manner in which these theories, concepts, and principles might be applied in other fields of endeavor. Unfortunately, the results of such developments made at the scientific and subsequent levels of exploration do not easily percolate through to the non-scientific community.

PARETO PRINCIPLE:

The Pareto Principle is very slowly gaining recognition as a useful tool for the business community. Scientists did not discover the Pareto Principle. Vilfredo Pareto was not a scientist. He was a sociologist, economist and philosopher. Joseph M. Juran, an Industrial Engineer, and others further expanded the application of the Pareto Principle. Widespread awareness, use, and acceptance of the Pareto Principle, as a tool in business, is yet to materialize. Unlike ENTROPY, here is a Principle that evolved outside of the scientific realm and thus far has received only slightly more recognition in the business community than the law of entropy.

PARKINSON'S LAW

C. Northcote Parkinson was a Naval Historian, Professor of History, and a prolific author. His most successful book, Parkinson's Law was published in 1958 in the United States. Parkinson's Law, which states: "Work expands to fill the time available for completion," has numerous secondary laws relating to expansion of elements into either time or space.

Parkinson's Law is the simplest, most observable, and most verifiable of the three universal principles presented here. As is the case with the previous two, this Law has not found its way into routine business practice.

Here we have three different universal laws principles, originating from different academic disciplines: Science - *Entropy*, Sociology, Economics, and Industrial Engineering - *Pareto Principle*, and History - *Parkinson's Law,* which seemingly, do not exist as far as the business world is concerned. I believe the origin of this failure by the business community to incorporate these laws/principles into their operational protocols lies in the *fundamental lack of recognition and awareness by business that all events in the universe are part of a process, governed by universal laws, and that there are no unique entities that exist apart from such governance.*

OTHER LAWS:

There are other universal laws that have application in business today, which generally are not being applied to any great extent. Two such examples are Chaos Theory and the Fibonacci Series.

CHAOS THEORY is the scientific investigation relating to the performance of Non-linear Systems. An increasing number of scientists worldwide continue the development of Chaos Theory, which currently has found applications in a wide range of disciplines such as biology, economics, finance, medicine, etc.[4]

FIBONACCI SERIES is a sequence of numbers: **0, 1, 1, 2, 3, 5, 8, 13, 21, 34, 55, 89,** which are found to occur in nature, human physiology, cosmology, the stock market, foreign exchange, etc. Although the continued development of the Fibonacci Series may not be apace with that of Chaos Theory, it is likely that future developments will lead to practical application of the Series in other non-scientific areas including business.

The business community will be have to search out applications from universal laws such as these, if they hope to achieve long term success in our modern technological world.

Now this is not the end. It is not even the beginning of the end. But it is perhaps, the end of the beginning.
Sir Winston Spenser Churchill[5] (1874-1965)

And those who were seen dancing were thought to be insane by those who could not hear the music.
Friedrich Nietzsche[6]

SUMMARY CONCLUSION:

ANOMIE: *n.* 1 instability in society caused by the erosion or abandonment of moral and social codes

AWARENESS: *adj.* 3 well informed about what is going on in the world or about the latest developments in a particular sphere of activity

COMMUNITY: *n.* 4 the public or society in general

IGNORANT: *adj.* 1 lacking knowledge and education in general or in a general or a specific subject
2 unaware of something
3 caused by lack of understanding or experience.

(Please note: What follows is based on my personal observations and experience. My observations are derived from analysis of decisions, actions, results, and consequences. I leave to others the luxury of judgment.)

A business is a community that exists in a local community that exists in a regional community that exists in a national community that exists in a global community. *Why don't we in business act like we are a part of the community instead of a unique and separate entity?* A business is a system. All systems in the universe are part of ongoing processes. Universal laws govern all processes. *Why don't we in business know this and operate our businesses congruent with universal laws?* A business is an organization of people interacting with people, and living in the community of people. *Why don't we in business value and treat our employees as our most important asset, and empower them to create success in the workplace on a daily basis?* The answer to all of the above is that the management of such business enterprises, as described above, is **_IGNORANT_**! This does not mean that all businesses operate in such a manner as portrayed, or that it is intentional. However, the larger the enterprise, the greater the possibility that this is so.

The word ignorant is used precisely but not derogatorily. If management is ignorant, *why?* Our society in this country today exists in a state of anomie. Look at today's modern cultural perspective in this country. We are an egocentric, fragmented, fear driven, frenetic society. Big is better: companies, buildings, cars, boats, etc. More is not enough! Communication has been degraded with the advent of the Internet and e-mail. Opinions, not facts, coupled with the insane mandate of political correctness are the order of the day. As a society, we are enamored with modern technology as the panacea for all of our ills. Modern technology is a two-sided coin, which encompasses the potential for both positive and negative consequences. Ignoring this reality is fraught with peril. The universe is held in balance by opposing but complementary forces. The ancient Chinese philosophers knew this when they spoke of Yin and Yang. All the universal laws are existent in balance with each other.

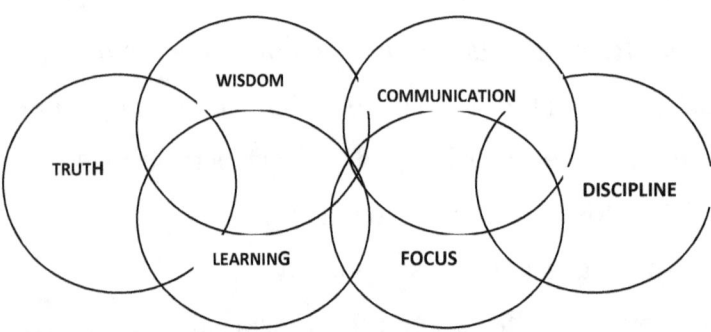

Illustration 7-1

Business today is a reflection of the society in which we live. The United States was once a recognized leader in the world community. Sadly this is no longer true. In order for business to break out of the miasma of today's society and segue to wholeness business must reconstruct itself from the ground up. A new paradigm, which encompasses basic fundamentals and universal principles, must be developed. The responsibility of the management team and the critical role of manager must be redefined in order to provide the leadership and direction required to accomplish this end. The manager, at whatever level of authority, must be a seeker of truth. Truth comes with the realization that an individual cannot accomplish what is required to be accomplished without the creative synergistic energy of those he/she is privileged to serve.

This book was intended to increase the awareness of the readers and point out that there is so much more to running a successful business than, perhaps, they have been exposed to in the past. Hopefully, the reader will be encouraged by this reading to seek further.

Thank you for letting me share my journey with you.

Refrences

PREFACE:

1 Albert Einstein, (1879-1955), Theoretical physicist.

2 IN SEARCH OF STONES... BY M. SCOTT PECK M.D.

3 Peter F. Drucker, (1909-): Writer, educator, and business consultant.

INTRODUCTION:

1 Hyman G. Rickover, (1900-1986), Admiral, United States Navy.

 "Father of the Nuclear Navy."

2 *THE ROCK, POEM, BY T. S. ELIOT*

3 *THE TRIPPING POINT* BY MALCOLM GLADWELL, CHAPTER 5 pp 178-181

CHAPTER ONE:

1 George Santayana, 1863-1952: Philosopher, essayist, poet, and
 novelist.

2 George Bernard Shaw, 1856-1950: Playwright, critic, and political activist.

3 Arthur Schopenhauer, 1788-1860: Philosopher

4 George Bernard Shaw

5 George Bernard Shaw

6 Internet: www.learningandteaching.info/learning/diddonance.htm

7 Herbert Spencer, 1820-1903: Philosopher, political theorist.

8 Chris Davis, www.ourworld.compuserve.com/homepage/cuius/idle/percept/blindspot.htm

9 ibid.

10 *THE ESSENCE OF WINNING AND LOSING* BY JOHN R. BOYD, January 1996

11 Albert Einstein

CHAPTER TWO:

1 Daniel Patrick Moynihan, 1927-2003, U. S. Senator from New York, Ambassador, socialist

2 *THE 80/20 PRINCIPLE,* CHAPTER 1, BY RIDHARD KOCH, 1950-, Management consultant, and entrepreneur. Part1,Chapter1,p.3

3 Vilfredo Pareto, 1848-1923: Sociologist, economist, and philosopher

4 Joseph M. Juran, 1904-, America Industrial Engineer,

philanthropist.

5 *PARKINSON'S LAWS BY C. NORTHCOTE PARKINSON*

CHAPTER THREE:

1 Ross Perot, 1930-, American businessman, billionaire

2 Peter F. Drucker, American, 1909-, (Austrian-born), Writer, educator and business consultant.

3 Caius Petronius 66 CE

4 Abraham H. Maslow, 1908-1970, American Psychologist

5 *FIASCO BY THOMAS E. RICKS*

6 Ross Perot

7 George Bernard Shaw, Man and Superman (1903) "Maxims for Revolutionists."

CHAPTER THREE, (cont.):

8 *GOOD TO GREAT: WHY SOME COMPANIES MAKE THE LEAP AND OTHERS DON'T BY JIM COLLINS*

9 Caesar Augustus, (Gaius Julius Caesar Octavianus), (63 BCE-14 CE) First Emperor of Rome

10 *MANAGING TRANSITIONS, 2nd edition, BY WILLIAM BRIDGES p.3*

11 www.measuringworth.com

CHAPTER FOUR:

1 Hyman G. Rickover

2 Confucius, (551-479 BCE) Chinese thinker, moral

philosopher.
3 Ralph Waldo Emerson, (1803-1882) American poet.
4 Robert Benchley, (1889-1945), Columnist, actor, screenwriter.

CHAPTER FIVE:
1 Erma Louise Bombeck, (1927-1996), "1f Life Is a Bowl of Cherries... 1971. American humorist.
2 Peter F. Drucker

CHAPTER SIX:
1 John Dewey, (1859-1952), US educator, pragmatist philosopher, psychologist.
2 Eric A. Burns, (1968-), "Gossamer Commons, 8/12/05" American critic, writer, poet, creator of WEBSNARK.
3 C.C. Krulak (1942-), General, U.S. Marine Corps, Commandant of the Marine Corps., Extract from John R. Boyd Eulogy, published by *Inside the Pentagon,* March 1997
4 WIKEPEDIA The Free Encyclopedia, OODA LOOP
5 *CERTAIN TO WIN BY CHET RICHARDS*

CHAPTER SEVEN:
1 Dietrich Bonhoeffer (1906-1945), German Lutheran Pastor, theologian. Executed by the Nazis in WWII.

2 *THE FABRIC OF THE COSMOS BY BRIAN GREENE* pp 150-159

3 *WIKEPEDIA* The Free Encyclopedia, The 2nd Law of Thermodynamics.

4 *WIKEPEDIA* The Free Encyclopedia, Chaos Theory.

5 Sir Winston Spencer Churchill (1874-1965), British politician,
 Prime Minister of the United Kingdom: May 1940- July 1945.

6 Friedrich Nietzsche, (1844-1900), German philosopher.

Recommended Reading

TITLE:	ISBN:	AUTHOR(S):
BUSINESS		
AUGUSTINE'S LAWS 6TH EDITION	1-56347-240-6	NORMAN R. AUGUSTINE
BLINK	0-316-17232-4	MALCOLM GLADWELL
CERTAIN TO WIN	1-4134-5376-7	CHET RICHARDS
FREAKONOMICS	978-0-061-23400-2	STEVEN D.LEVITT, STEPHEN J. DUBNER
GOOD TO GREAT:...	978-0-066-62099-2	JIM COLLINS
MANAGING TRANSITIONS 2ND EDITION	0-7382-0824-8	WILLIAM BRIDGES
MORAL MAZES	0-19-506080-6	ROBERT JACKALL
PARKINSON'S LAW	1-56849-015-1	C. NORTHCOTE PARKINSON
POWERSHIFT	0-553-29215-3	ALVIN TOFFLER
QUALITY IS FREE	0-451-62585-4	PHILIP B. CROSBY
SUPER CRUNCHERS	978-0-553-80540-6	IAN AYRES
THE 80/20 PRINCIPLE	0-385-49174-3	RICHARD KOCH
THE ETERNALLY SUCCESSFUL ORGANIZ.	0-451-62846-2	PHILIP B. CROSBY

THE PETER PRINCIPLE	1-56849-161-1	LAURENCE J.PETER, RAYMOND HULL
THE PETER PYRAMID	0-553-26347-1	LAURENCE J. PETER
THE STARFISH AND THE SPIDER	1-59184-143-7	ORI BRAFMAN, ROD A.BECKSTROM
THE TRIPPING POINT	0-316-34662-4	MALCOLM GLADWELL
THE WISDOM OF CROWDS	0-385-72170-6	JAMES SUROWIECKI

SCIENCE		
CHAOS	0-14-009250-1	JAMES GLEICK
SEVEN LIFE LESSONS OF CHAOS	0-06-018246-6	JOHN BRIGGS, F.DAVID PEAT
THE DANCING WU LI MASTERS	0-553-26382-X	GARY ZUKAV
THE FABRIC OF THE COSMOS	0-375-72720-5	BRIAN GREENE
THE TAO OF PHYSICS	1-57062-519-0	FRITJOF CAPRA
WHOLENESS AND THE IMPLICATE ORDER	0-415-11966-9	DAVID BOHM

MILITARY		
BOYD	0-316-88146-5	ROBERT CORAM
FIASCO	1-59420-103-X	THOOMAS E RICKS
SUN TZU THE ART OF WAR	0-19-501476-6	SAMUEL B. GRIFFITH
THE MARINE CORPS WAY	0-07-142377-X	SANTAMARIA, MARTINO, CLEMONS
THE MIND OF WAR	1-58834-178-X	GRANT T. HAMMOND
THE PASSION OF COMMAND	0-940328-37-2	COL B.P. MCCOY, USMC
WARFIGHTING	0-385-	GENERAL A. M. GRAY, USMC

	47834-8	
GENERAL		
AMERICAN EDUC.A NATIONAL FAILURE	63-15788	H.G. RICKOVER USN
THE WISDOM OF INSECURITY	0-394-70468-1	ALAN W. WATTS
REFERENCE		
ELEMENTARY LOGIC	0-674-24451-6	WILLIAM VANORMAN QUINE

Acknowledgments

The question of whether the Acknowledgements for this book should be presented in the beginning of the book or at the close of the book was not the primary question for me to confront. My question was: Does anybody ever care about, or read the acknowledgements at all? Lacking definitive proof, one way or another, and deeming it important for me to express my thanks to those people who made the writing of this book possible, whether anyone reads the acknowledgements or not, or for that matter the book or not here we are:

Life should be an ongoing learning experience and this requires awareness and willingness on the part of an individual to pursue learning and the knowledge it brings every day, without fail. In this regard then, all of the people I have encountered in my journey through life thus far have been my teachers; for this lesson was imparted to me as a child by my Father, Francis Collins. My Father came to this country as an immigrant at the age of 29 years, having survived the savagery of more than two years of combat on the Western Front, in the British Army in the Great War. He had a 5th grade education, having had to leave school to work in the coal mines in Scotland, with his Father to help support his family. My Father, who became a U.S. citizen at age 39 years, through hard work, self-education, and the opportunities found in this country became the first person in the history of his family to own an automobile and purchase a home. My Father had an insatiable desire to learn, which was one of the many gifts he gave to me.

Mel Zenphenning was the second Foreman, (Foreman was the position title given to first line supervisors in a simpler time), I was assigned to work under in the early days of my Electrical Apprenticeship at an automobile assembly plant in Detroit, Michigan. After the introductions were made, Mel asked me if I wanted to learn, or did I want to drink coffee and fuck around like the other Apprentices. When I told Mel that I was there to learn, he took me under his wing, and for the next two years taught me how to design electrical control circuits. At the time Mel, in addition to his Foreman position at the plant, owned and operated a successful Electrical Design Company in the Detroit area. Mel taught me a very valuable lesson: One of the primary duties of anyone in a supervisory position, lead man to manager, was to teach and to train those under their charge.

Howard Roberts was the Manager for whom I worked, for three years, in my first executive manager's position with a Detroit, Michigan, Defense Contractor. During that time period I watched Howard solve complex plant operational problems through the simple technique of listening intently to all sides before coming to a decision and presenting an action plan to effectively deal with the problem. When he was listening, one might think in observing Howard's posture and demeanor, that he was asleep while the conversations, and oftentimes controversy, swirled around him. However, whenever everyone was finished talking, Howard would pause for a few minutes before speaking, and then he would succinctly summarize the various positions presented, present his conclusions, and delineate the action plan to deal with the issue. Howard was a master at this. Howard was very seldom off base in the decisions that he made. Howard, more than anyone else, taught me the value of listening, listening, listening, and then listening some more to all sides of a discussion before coming to a conclusion and decision as to how then to proceed.

Herman Archer was the Assistant Project Director for whom I worked as a Plant Facility Supervisor on a major construction project in the Middle East. Herman was a consummate professional in all aspects of Project Management. Herman was superbly educated with an advanced degree in Civil Engineering, and degrees in Construction Finance, Labor Relations, Political Science, plus more than 30 years field experience in running major construction projects in Africa, the Middle East, and the

United States. From Herman, I learned organization, focus, and simple, yet highly effective, approaches to planning, execution, and problem solving.

Bob Hiller was the President and part owner of an Industrial Construction Company, where I worked for Bob on two separate occasions, some 5 years apart. From Bob I was given an entrance to the perspective of the Entrepreneur: creative visionary, risk taker, energy charged, and dynamic personality. For me, this was a whole new world, one that my own personality precludes me from ever entering.

First, last, and foremost, I owe a great debt to my Beloved Wife, Colleen for her encouragement, continuous support, critical judgment, and an unrelenting desire on her part to read "short sentences."

And to all the unnamed, thank you for your encouragement and support.

www.ingramcontent.com/pod-product-compliance
Lightning Source LLC
Chambersburg PA
CBHW080659190526

45169CB00006B/2186